Let My People Go

AFRICAN AMERICANS
1804–1860

THE YOUNG OXFORD HISTORY OF
AFRICAN AMERICANS

Robin D.G. Kelley and Earl Lewis
General Editors

Let My People Go

◇ ◇ ◇

AFRICAN AMERICANS
1804–1860

DEBORAH GRAY WHITE

Oxford University Press
New York • Oxford

In memory of Cathy Belinda Taylor

Oxford University Press

Oxford   New York
Athens Auckland Bangkok Bombay
Calcutta Cape Town Dar es Salaam Delhi
Florence Hong Kong Istanbul Karachi
Kuala Lumpur Madras Madrid Melbourne
Mexico City Nairobi Paris Singapore
Taipei Tokyo Toronto
and associated companies in
Berlin   Ibadan

Published by Oxford University Press, Inc.,
198 Madison Avenue, New York, New York 10016
Oxford is a registered trademark of Oxford University Press

Library of Congress Cataloging-in-Publication Data
White, Deborah Gray
Let my people go—African Americans, 1804–1860 / Deborah Gray White
p. cm. — (The young Oxford history of African Americans : vol. 4)
Includes bibliographical references and index.
ISBN 0-19-508769-0 (library ed.); ISBN 0-19-508502-7 (series, lib. ed.)
1. Slavery—Southern States—History—19th century—Juvenile literature.
2. Afro-Americans—History—To 1863—Juvenile literature.
[1. Slavery. 2. Afro-Americans—History—To 1863.]
I. Title. II. Series.
E185.Y68   1995
[E446]
973'.0496073 s—dc20
[975'.0496073]   95-38104
CIP

1 3 5 7 9 8 6 4 2

Printed in the United States of America
on acid-free paper

Design: Sandy Kaufman
Layout: Loraine Machlin
Picture research: Lisa Kirchner, Laura Kreiss

On the cover: A Southern Cornfield, Nashville, Tenn. (1861), Thomas Waterman Wood.
Frontispiece: A slave market in Atlanta.
Page 11: Detail from *The Contribution of the Negro to Democracy in America,* (1943)
by Charles White, 11'9" x17'3". Hampton University Museum, Hampton, Virginia.

CONTENTS

◇ ◇ ◇

INTRODUCTION—
ROBIN D. G. KELLEY AND EARL LEWIS 7

Chapter 1
THE RISE OF COTTON 13

Chapter 2
WHAT SLAVERY WAS 25

Chapter 3
SLAVE COMMUNITIES 39

Chapter 4
FIT FOR FREEDOM 57

Chapter 5
A DIFFERENT KIND OF FREEDOM 73

Chapter 6
LET MY PEOPLE GO 99

Chapter 7
FROM DESPERATION TO HOPE 117

CHRONOLOGY 136

FURTHER READING 138

INDEX 140

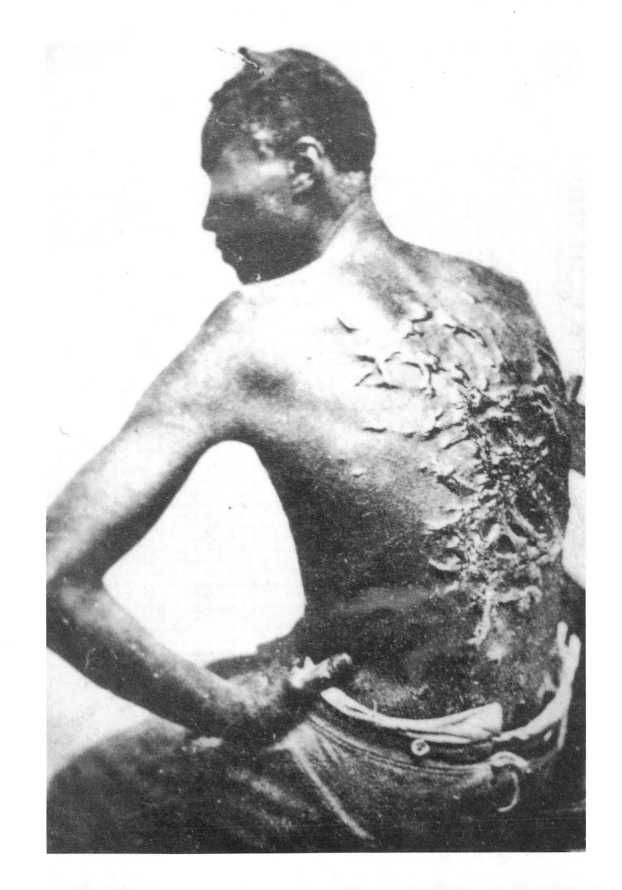

ROBIN D. G. KELLEY
EARL LEWIS

INTRODUCTION

The folk tales that slaves passed down to their children and grandchildren are more than quaint stories about weaker animals using their cunning to overcome the powerful, or moral tales that teach the difference between good and evil. These age-old stories often contain rich insights into history. The slaves of the Georgia Sea Islands, for instance, used to tell a funny tale about a master who forced his mule to work on Sunday. This practice went on for several weeks until one day the tired and disgusted mule turned to his master and began protesting in clear, eloquent English. "Great Gawd," said the master, who by now was scared out of his wits, "I never seen a mule talk before!" A dog who was sitting under a shade tree nearby replied, "Me neither." Of course, these talking animals frightened the master, who willingly yielded to the mule's demand for Sundays off.

The most obvious moral of the story is that slaves, too, must follow the Biblical injunction against working on the Sabbath. A less obvious but equally important purpose of the story is to show what happens when the master learns that his "mules"—meaning his slaves—not only talk but protest the conditions of their enslavement. Of course, from our vantage point almost a century and a half later, the fact that slaves had voices and used them should not surprise us. But it often surprised their owners since many convinced themselves that enslaved Africans could be "broken" like horses and that deep down they were docile people put on this earth to serve the "white race." At least that is what many masters claimed to believe. The truth is, they were also scared of their imprisoned black laborers, which is why they used whips and chains to keep

The scars on the back of this former slave serve as a reminder of the cruel legacy of slavery.

them in line, developed elaborate systems to police the plantations, and passed a flurry of laws intended to keep both the slave and free black populations under control. The free black community was considered especially dangerous to the slave masters. Although legal and informal discrimination sharply restricted their voices and activity, free African-Americans had much more space to maneuver, to build community institutions, and to speak out against the evils of slavery than their sisters and brothers in bondage.

The era from 1800 to the Civil War, also known as the antebellum period, in some ways parallels the folk tale from the Georgia Sea Islands. It was a period when black voices against slavery became even more intense. Free and enslaved African-Americans, including notable figures like Gabriel Prosser, Denmark Vesey, and Nat Turner, attempted to launch slave rebellions against the system. David Walker, Frederick Douglass, Maria Stewart, Henry Highland Garnet, and a host of others, wrote militant books, pamphlets, and speeches calling for the abolition of slavery and condemning the United States for its hypocritical claim to being a "land of the free." Indeed, the rising voices of black, as well as white, abolitionists is partly responsible for the eradication of slavery in the Northern states during the early 19th century.

Black voices and actions certainly surprised the masters, but unlike the planter in our tale, real-life plantation owners were unwilling to yield. As the industrial revolution got underway in the Northeastern states and England, the market for cotton was more profitable than ever. And after inventor Eli Whitney created a machine that could easily re-move the seeds from cotton bolls—a slow and tedious chore slaves had to do by hand—plantation owners were able to grow even more cotton with less hands. So they were not about to give up the slave system so easily. Even after the United States abolished the slave trade in 1808, plantation owners in the less fertile "upper South" added a new twist to the business of human bondage by breeding their slaves like cattle and selling them to the growing cotton plantations of the South and South-west.

This book documents the growing tension between the African-American struggle to be free—and remain free—in the United States, and the slaveholders' efforts to keep the system alive and profitable. *Let My People Go* not only details what slavery was like for men, women, and

This early form of mass transit, powered by a horse and a slave with a whip, could carry up to 12 passengers.

children imprisoned in white homes and plantations, but how they created communities under bondage, how they fought back, and how they contributed to the system's decline. The book also documents the making of "free" black communities in a land where the vast majority of their sisters and brothers were slaves. As historian Deborah Gray White demonstrates, the central goal of free blacks in antebellum America, beyond their very survival as a people, was to fight for the complete abolition of slavery. And fight they did, often in concert with fellow slaves, sometimes in alliance with progressive white abolitionists, sometimes all alone. Without the efforts of slaves and free blacks, the history of slavery's demise would look very different.

This book is part of an 11-volume series that narrates African-American history from the 15th through the 20th centuries. Since the 1960s, a rapid explosion in research on black Americans has significantly modified previous understanding of that experience. Studies of slavery, African-American culture, social protest, families, and religion, for example, silenced those who had previously labeled black Americans insignificant historical actors. This new research followed a general upsurge of interest in the social and cultural experiences of the supposedly powerless men and women who did not control the visible reins of power. The result has been a careful and illuminating portrait of how ordinary people make history and serve as the architects of their own destinies.

This series explores many aspects of the lives of African Americans. It describes how blacks shaped and changed the history of this nation. It also places the lives of African Americans in the context of the Americas as a whole. We start the story more than a century before the day in 1619 when 19 "negars" stepped off a Spanish ship in Jamestown, Virginia, and end with the relationship between West Indian immigrants and African Americans in large urban centers like New York in the late 20th century.

At the same time, the series addresses a number of interrelated questions: What was life like for the first Africans to land in the Americas, and what were the implications for future African Americans? Were all Africans and African Americans enslaved? How did race shape slavery and how did slavery influence racism? The series also considers questions about male-female relationships, the forging of African-American communities, religious beliefs and practices, the experiences of the young, and the changing nature of social protest. The key events in American history are here, too, but viewed from the perspective of African Americans. The result is a fascinating and compelling story of nearly five centuries of African-American history.

THE YOUNG OXFORD HISTORY OF
AFRICAN AMERICANS

Volume 1
THE FIRST PASSAGE
BLACKS IN THE AMERICAS 1502–1617

Volume 2
STRANGE NEW LAND
AFRICAN AMERICANS 1617–1776

Volume 3
REVOLUTIONARY CITIZENS
AFRICAN AMERICANS 1776–1804

Volume 4
LET MY PEOPLE GO
AFRICAN AMERICANS 1804–1860

Volume 5
BREAK THOSE CHAINS AT LAST
AFRICAN AMERICANS 1860–1880

Volume 6
THOUGH JUSTICE SLEEPS
AFRICAN AMERICANS 1880–1900

Volume 7
A CHANCE TO MAKE GOOD
AFRICAN AMERICANS 1900–1929

Volume 8
FROM A RAW DEAL TO A NEW DEAL?
AFRICAN AMERICANS 1929–1945

Volume 9
WE CHANGED THE WORLD
AFRICAN AMERICANS 1945–1970

Volume 10
INTO THE FIRE
AFRICAN AMERICANS SINCE 1970

Volume 11
BIOGRAPHICAL SUPPLEMENT
AND INDEX

CHAPTER 1

THE RISE OF COTTON

◇ ◇ ◇

O n August 30 in the year 1800, a chilling fear spread among the white people of Henrico County, Virginia. Within a few days the fear had gripped the minds of most white Virginians. Within weeks, slaveholders as far west and south as what was then the Mississippi Territory were cautioning each other to beware of suspicious behavior on the part of blacks. On their tongues was the name Gabriel Prosser; in their minds were thoughts of what might have happened if Prosser had succeeded in leading Virginia slaves in revolt against slavery.

Prosser, his wife Nanny, and his two brothers, Martin and Solomon, were a slaveholder's nightmare. Born into slavery, they declared themselves fit for freedom. They decided not only that they would be free but that all slaves should be free. Together they plotted to lead the slaves of the Richmond area in revolt against the city. Their plan was to capture the arsenal and, once supplied with weapons, to take over Richmond and then other cities in the state. Virginia, it was planned, would become a free state, a black state, a homeland for those unfit for slavery.

But Prosser never got a chance to put his plan into action. On the night of the scheduled attack on Richmond, a terrible storm washed out the bridges and roads to the city. Prosser had to postpone his rebellion, and the delay gave someone time to betray him and expose the plan. All who conspired in the revolt were captured and put to death. Gabriel was among the last to be captured, tried, and hanged.

Working in the fields from sunup to sundown, these slaves were forced to endure a world of constant toil.

Ten Dollars Reward.

RANAWAY on the twelfth day of April laft, *GABRIEL*, a flave the property of Mrs Mary Bolling, of Peterfburg; obtained leave of abfence for 15 days to go to Mr. Benjamin Marable's in Gloucefter County—and the faid flave not having returned yet, and there being good reafon to believe that he is ftill lurking in that neighbourhood—the above fum will be paid for having him confined in jail fo that his owner gets him again, or a reward of Twenty Dollars, exclufive of what the law allows if brought home. Gabriel is a black man, about 30 years old, long vifage, about 6 feet high, fond of drink, and by trade a weaver. He was purchafed from the eftate of the late Colonel Peyton, and is well known in that part of the country. All perfons are forewarned from harbouring, employing or carrying the faid fellow out of the State.

Richeson Booker.

Peterfburg, October 30, 1800. eotf

The Richmond Examiner *posted this notice for a runaway slave named Gabriel on November 4, 1800.*

He was, however, one of the first people in the 19th century to struggle in the name of freedom. And this is really the theme of this period of African-American history: the fight against slavery, the struggle to be free American citizens, and resistance, despite incredible odds, to maintain human dignity in the face of overwhelming inhumanity. The chance that the African Americans would succeed was small. The odds against it being a bloodless struggle were overwhelming. And those odds increased after cotton became this country's principal export crop.

Before the 1790s slavery seemed to be a dying institution. Most northern states had set emancipation in motion, and in the Chesapeake states of Virginia, Maryland, and Delaware, the philosophy of the American Revolution—the idea that all men were created equal, with the right to life, liberty, and the pursuit of happiness—also motivated planters to free their slaves. Of crucial importance to manumission, or the act of freeing slaves, in the Chesapeake was the decline of tobacco. Years of overplanting had left the lands worn out, and recovery from the destruction of the Revolutionary War was slow. As farmers produced less tobacco and turned instead to more profitable grains, their need for large numbers of slaves decreased. Rather than assume the cost of caring for their slaves, many farmers freed them instead.

But the introduction of cotton, which increased the demand for slaves south of the Chesapeake, caused a hurried change in attitude. Before the turn of the 19th century, rice, corn, hemp, indigo, tobacco, and grains were grown in the South, but there was little cotton production. Only the long-staple variety was cultivated. Silky and delicate, with a seed that was not easily separated from the long fibers, long-staple cotton was temperamental and required just the right kind of soil and weather. Since the proper conditions existed only on the Sea Islands off the coast of South Carolina and Georgia, cotton production was limited.

Eli Whitney's cotton gin changed that, and with it also the history of black America. For what the cotton gin did was make the production of a heartier short-staple cotton profitable. The gin allowed the sticky seed of this seldom-grown cotton to be separated from its coarse fibers with ease. Before the invention of the cotton gin it took a slave a day to clean a pound of short-staple cotton; it was a laborious chore to remove the seed from the fiber. With a gin, by contrast, the slave could clean up to 50 pounds in a day.

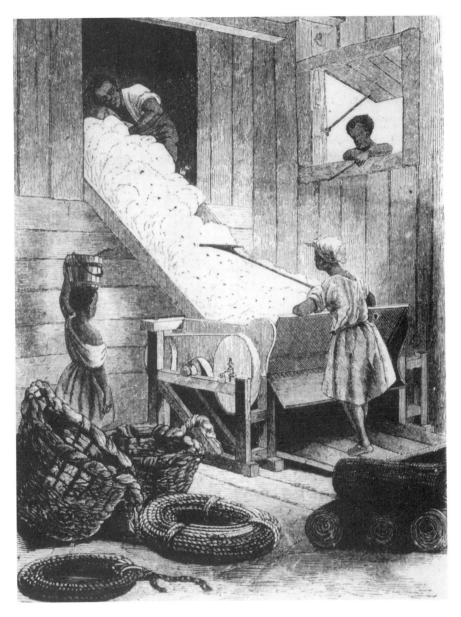

By making cotton a profitable crop for Southern farmers, the cotton gin increased the demand for slaves and changed the course of history for black Americans.

Short-staple cotton also had the advantage of not being so delicate. It could be, and was, planted all over the land south of Virginia. And it was in demand throughout the world, especially in England, where textile manufacturers never seemed to get enough. It was not long before cotton became the principal cash crop of the South and of the nation. In 1790 the South produced only 3,135 bales of cotton. By 1800 this figure had grown to 73,145 bales; by 1820 output amounted to 334,378 bales, accounting for more than half of the nation's agricultural exports. On the eve of the Civil War, production peaked at 4.8 million bales. If ever circumstances conspired against a people, it was the coming together of the cotton gin, short-staple cotton, fertile lands, and world demand. Once this happened, slaves who might have been set free by debt and conscience-ridden Chesapeake planters were instead sold to the planters of the cotton-growing states of the Lower South. Cotton sealed the fate of slaves and slavery.

It seemed as though Gabriel Prosser knew this. Like so many other blacks, he probably saw slaveholders close down their Virginia tobacco farms and plantations and head with their slaves south and west toward the fertile black soil of the soon-to-be cotton belt. Like others, he no doubt winced at the sight of chained slaves heading out of the declining economies of Virginia, Maryland, and South Carolina to the booming areas of Alabama, Mississippi, Louisiana, Arkansas, and Texas. In 1800 these areas were not even states. Texas, in fact, was still part of Mexico. These places were not uninhabited, but were home to five Native American tribes, the Creeks, Choctaws, Seminoles, Chickasaws, and Cherokees. No matter, though. The certain wealth that cotton brought ensured that these areas would soon be flooded with white settlers who would see to it that the land became theirs. They would turn the territories into states and in the process transform the very nature of slavery.

Essential to the transformation was the domestic slave trade. Before 1800 a slave stood some chance of obtaining his or her freedom, either through self-purchase, meritorious service, or simply through the good will of a master or mistress; after 1800 the increased profitability of slavery made manumission for an individual slave less likely. Once cotton gave slavery a new lease on life, slaves who were of no use in the Upper South were not set free, but sold to the Lower South. This meant that a good many of the slaves born in Virginia, Maryland, or South Carolina were likely to die in Mississippi, Alabama, or Louisiana. The domestic trade established the means of getting them there. At the same time that slaves lived in fear of having their families torn apart and being "sold down the river," domestic slave traders calculated just how much able-bodied field hands, especially those between the ages of 15 and 25, sold for in the new markets.

The sale and transportation of black people within the United States thus became big business. What had once taken place mostly on the African continent—the theft of people, the rending of families—now took place with vulgar regularity before the eyes and ears of American whites and blacks. From Virginia alone, an estimated 300,000 slaves were transported south for sale between 1830 and 1860. As the slave pens sprung up, so too did the sights and sounds of human misery. Within view of the nation's capitol were slave pens that were, as kidnapped slave Solomon Northup described them, constructed so that "the outside world could never see the human cattle that were herded there." Within the walls of the pens, in open-air dirt yards, and on the auction blocks, slave husbands and wives were separated from each other, parents were parted from their children, and infants were torn from their mothers' breasts. Free blacks, too, feared the trade, for like Northup they could be, and were, stolen by unscrupulous traders anxious to make money by any means. Blacks, who once had hoped that the constitutional provision for the ending of the slave trade in 1808 would put slavery on the road to extinction, now knew that slavery was not about to die.

In fact, the new lease on life that the cotton gin gave slavery changed things dramatically. Take, for instance, free-black men and women, people like Philadelphia sailmaker James Forten or abolitionist Maria Stewart. Always an anomaly in a society where dark skin color was a badge of bondage, free blacks became even more insecure with the transformation of slavery. First and foremost, the newly revitalized institution of slavery decreased their numbers. This meant that the free-black population would always remain small, with limited ability to affect the course of slavery. Free blacks always had to protect themselves against kidnappers. Those who made up the small communities of southern free blacks had to keep their free papers close or else be mistaken for slaves. In both the North and South free blacks found it beneficial to have white friends who could testify on their behalf should they be mistaken as slaves. The long and the short of it was that the transformation of slavery put free blacks at risk.

What it did to those in bondage was much worse. Their loss was very personal, because throughout the Upper South their families were torn apart. Whites who migrated to the Lower South went in family groups. Those who did not were usually single men who chose to seek

> ## TO SLAVE OWNERS.
>
> TWO gentlemen in Louisiana, wishing to enlarge their planting interest, would purchase for this purpose entire gangs of SLAVES, of not less than forty or fifty, to the number of one hundred and fifty. Large slave owners, who may wish to sell out, or to diminish their numbers, by selling in a lot where they will be kept together, can communicate with the advertiser by addressing, through the Post Office, at Richmond, Box No. 458, or John A. Parker, Esq., Tappahannoek, Essex County, Va., where information can be obtained of the parties and of their views.
>
> If preferred, contracts would be entered into this Spring, and possession of the slaves retained until October next.   May 11—ctt

Two plantation owners in Louisiana, seeking to expand their business, placed this advertisement in the Richmond Enquirer.

their fortune in the new area. Slaves had no choice. They were taken or sold against their will, forced to leave family, friends, and all that was familiar. Lost to each other forever, family members separated by hundreds of miles suffered tremendous grief. Said one slave when he was sold from Tennessee to Louisiana: "I lost my people and I'm never going to see them no more in this world." And he never did.

More than likely, the work that this slave did in Louisiana was a lot harder than what he had done in Tennessee. By the time cotton production began to soar in the states of the Lower South, Virginia, Maryland, North Carolina, and South Carolina were considered "old" states. The land had long been cleared of brush and trees, farms and plantations had already been built, fields had been readied for crops, roads made transportation and communication easy, cities made commercial and cultural exchange possible.

The Lower South was not so "civilized." All the work that had been done in the Upper South had to be repeated here. It was the new frontier, and as on all frontiers the work was more backbreaking. To Adeline Cunningham, an ex-slave from Texas, everything was hard. As she put it: "Dey was rough people and dey treat ev'ry body rough." Evidence of

A slave auction house in Alexandria, Virginia.

rough treatment could be found in the slaves' birth and death rates. Compared with African Americans in other regions in the United States, blacks in the Lower South did not live as long nor have as many children.

And yet, for all of the terrible changes that took place in the first few decades of the 19th century, the overall condition of the average slave actually improved. This is one of the great paradoxes of the history of bondage in America. As slavery became more entrenched, as more families were separated and freedom became less attainable, it actually got better in terms of physical treatment. In the 19th century there were far less brandings that marked slaves as personal property. Limb amputations for theft and running away were curtailed and disabling whippings and murder occurred less frequently. Work was still back-breaking and endless, punishment was still certain, but more attention was paid to diet, slaves were given more personal time, and marital life was encouraged.

The reasons for these seemingly contrary occurrences are easy to understand. They were the consequence of the closing of the international slave trade at the very time that cotton made slavery profitable. Once it was no longer possible to bring slaves from Africa, slaveholders were forced to treat the slaves they had better. They needed slaves for work, and so they needed to keep the slaves they had healthy and productive—and they needed those slaves to reproduce themselves.

This need resulted in better material conditions for African Americans held in bondage. Even given the severe conditions on the frontier, in comparison with Africans held in slavery in Brazil, Cuba, and Puerto Rico, American slaves lived longer. Of critical importance was the high rate of fertility—the birth rate—in the United States. Out of all the slaveholding countries in the Western Hemisphere, only in the United States did this happen. The better living conditions that caused the higher fertility rates developed out of greed and intense disregard for African-American humanity—negative qualities, but ones that helped the African-American community grow. Only here was the ratio of slave men to women relatively equal, and only here did families develop. Only here did this result in the creation of what has been termed "the slave community."

The slaveholder was, however, driven more by the profit motive than interest in the communities developed by slaves. Certainly African Americans survived better in comparison to Africans in other Western Hemisphere regions, but the lives of black Americans, compared to that of other Americans, was hard, intolerable, and unprotected. Everything about slavery went against every principle upon which the nation was founded. In slavery there was no liberty, no equality, no democracy. It therefore needed justification. A reason had to be found to explain why slavery existed in the nation that was the most free in the world. A reason was needed to excuse the South and ease the conscience of the individual slaveholder.

In the pro-slavery argument was every excuse upon which the South built its institution. At its center was denial of the worth of the African American. Blacks, the argument went, were everything but prepared for freedom. They were childlike, in need of direction. They were lazy people who would not work if not forced to. They were cursed by

THE NEGRO IN HIS OWN COUNTRY.

THE NEGRO IN AMERICA.

Two engravings from the Bible Defence of Slavery *(1853). Many Southern slave owners believed that blacks benefited from slavery.*

God, and slavery was God's punishment. They were, some insisted, so unlike whites that they were a different species. In short, the pro-slavery argument turned slavery into something that at its worst was a necessary evil, and at its best a positive good.

Slavery was good for the South, good for black people, and good for the nation, or so the argument went. When William Harper, Chancellor of the University of South Carolina, wrote about slavery he declared that blacks "are undergoing the very best education which it is possible to give. They are in the course of being taught habits of regular and patient industry, and this is the first lesson that is required."

Like Harper, pro-slavery writers generally overlooked or denied the brutality of slavery. Most insisted that cruelty occurred only in the rarest of instances. Most also believed that their slaves lived better than the average industrial worker, including those in the northern United States. Factory owners, it was argued, cared nothing for their laborers. In contrast to Northern and European "wage slaves" who were worked until they were of no use to the company, after which they were fired to fend for themselves, southern slaves received free food, clothing, housing, and medical care for life. A typical opinion on this matter was expressed by Virginia Baptist minister Thorton Springfellow. Like most slaveholders, he believed that the slaves' "condition . . . is now better than that of any equal number of laborers on earth, and is daily improving."

Obviously, Gabriel Prosser and his followers thought differently. To them slavery was not a kind and caring institution but a malicious one that robbed them of their freedom. Their feelings were shared by both free and enslaved African Americans, all of whom struggled in one way or another against slavery, all of whom at one time or another raised the plaintive cry: "Let my people go."

CHAPTER 2
WHAT SLAVERY WAS

◇ ◇ ◇

In the South, before the Civil War, the year began the same way as it ended—with work in cotton. During January and February slaves finished ginning and pressing cotton, and hauled it in wagons to the point of shipment. In March and April they were ready to start planting again. It took at least three slaves to plant a row of cotton. One slave drove a mule and plowed through the dirt to break the land into a row. A young slave came behind dropping the seed into the ground, followed by another slave with another mule-drawn plow, covering up the seed. Between April and August, the cotton was plowed and hoed by slaves, first to make sure that there was only one stalk of cotton to what was called a hill, then to keep the land free of weeds and grass. In late August, slaves began the cotton-picking season. Unmercifully long, it lasted through January of the next year.

Slaves who cultivated rice, tobacco, hemp, or sugar had a similar year-round routine, and like those who worked in cotton, their work did not end with the sale of the crop. There were hogs to kill, and then the meat had to be cut and salted. New land was cleared. Ditches were dug, cleaned, and repaired. Fences were built and under constant repair, wood was cut and hauled, and vegetable gardens were cultivated. On top of all this was the cultivation of corn, a crop that needed extensive hoeing, plowing, and harvesting just like the cash crop.

The slaves' day did not end when fieldwork was done. At night men cut wood while women prepared meals, spun thread, wove cloth, and made clothes. On Saturday afternoons men often trapped while women

Picking cotton on a Georgia plantation. Slaves who failed to meet their quota were punished.

25

washed clothes, made candles and soap, and helped the men tend the garden plots where they grew the few vegetables they ate.

Slaves whose chores were in the master's house worked as much as field hands. Besides taking care of their own families, and doing their cooking, cleaning, sewing, and washing, they did all of the domestic tasks, day and night, for the slave master's family.

For the slave this added up to endless work. But that is what slavery was, a system of forced labor in which the African American worked without pay for someone else's profit. Everything else derived from slavery was secondary to this central point. For instance, this system of forced labor provided slaveholders with the wealth and prestige that they needed to dominate southern politics and social relations. Further, slavery organized the races not only to separate blacks and whites, but to give *all* whites status simply because they were white, and to deny status to *all* blacks simply because they were black. An example of how inhumane one group of people could be to another, slavery was also one of

After a long day in the fields, women still had to tend to their families' needs. Here, slave women dry laundry in their Virginia cabin.

the main causes of the Civil War, the bloodiest conflict ever fought on American soil.

As a system of labor that exploited black work, slavery usually benefitted a white man, but sometimes the slave master was a white woman, a Native American, or rarely, a black man or woman. Ultimately, the nation prospered from this exploitation, because as the South grew rich off the cultivation of cash crops, so did the country as a whole. The losers were the African Americans who lost their freedom. Their loss was never as complete as the slaveholder wanted, but it was complete enough to organize African-American life around endless work whose rewards always went to someone else.

Wherever one went in the South between 1800 and 1860 one could expect to see slaves doing some kind of work. They worked as lumberjacks and turpentine producers in the forests of the Carolinas and Georgia. In Virginia and Kentucky, slaves worked in the gold, coal, and salt mines. On the Mississippi River steamboats they worked as deckhands and boiler stokers. In Georgia and Louisiana they worked as textile laborers. Slave labor was so profitable that in 1847 the owners of the Tredegar Iron Works in Richmond, Virginia, shifted from using white laborers to slave labor. In addition to serving as factory laborers, slaves also made up a significant portion of the South's skilled artisans—carpenters, coopers, blacksmiths, silversmiths, and the like.

However, most of the 4 million African Americans who were enslaved in 1860 worked in the fields of the farms and plantations of the South. They worked on an average day 14 hours in the summer and 10 hours in the winter. During harvest time slaves often worked 18-hour days in sun that was piercing, heat that was sweltering.

Needless to say, their work was backbreaking. The average slave worked in cotton production, and during harvest season was expected to pick about 130 to 150 pounds of cotton per day. Work in sugar and rice was equally hard, if not harder. Both crops demanded constant cultivation and the digging of drainage ditches in snake-infested fields. At harvest time on the sugar plantations, slaves had to cut, strip, and carry cane to the sugar house for boiling. This was extremely strenuous work. Rice cultivation was even more miserable. Since rice is grown under water, slaves spent long hours standing in water up to their knees.

With so much wealth riding on it, slave work was hardly done haphazardly. On the contrary, it was carefully organized so that slaves worked either in gangs or according to tasks. Slave work gangs usually did as much work as the fastest worker could do. The task system provided greater flexibility, and although assignments were as taxing as those done by gangs, when a slave or a group of slaves finished the assigned task, they could quit work for the day. Unlike the gang system, in which men and women usually worked in separate groups, tasks were often assigned to a family.

Slaves who worked in the house had a totally different regimen, one that was physically easier but mentally taxing. Women predominated in the house, and like male slave artisans, they did work that allowed for more creativity and self-direction than the work done by field hands. Working indoors, they cooked, cleaned, did laundry, sewed, and cared for infants. Although they could count on better food and clothing than their counterparts in the field, they were under closer supervision, were on call both day and night, and were more often involved in personality

Producing turpentine in the woods of South Carolina. In the South, virtually every type of industry relied on slave labor.

Scales like this one were used to measure each slave's production in the cotton fields.

conflicts with the white family. As put by one house servant, "We were constantly exposed to the whims and passions of every member of the family." This meant everything from assignment to petty jobs to insults, spontaneous angry whippings, and sexual assaults.

Although house servants were under the closest surveillance, compared to slaves in other parts of the Americas all slaves in the United States were relatively closely supervised. Unlike in Caribbean slave societies or in Latin America, slaves, slaveholders, and overseers in the United States lived in very close proximity to each other. In Jamaica, for instance, one-third of all slaves lived on estates with 200 slaves or more, and three-quarters of all slaves lived on holdings of at least 50. Such large numbers of bondsmen made close supervision of slave life and work impossible.

In the United States, by contrast, such large plantations were rare. Only one-quarter of all slaves lived on plantations with more than 50 slaves. Since most lived on holdings of 10 to 49 slaves, and about one-quarter lived on very small holdings of 1 to 9 slaves, slave work and life was constantly monitored and supervised so that masters could reap every bit of profit they thought they were entitled to.

Slaves were not unaware of how hard they worked and how unfortunate their condition was. John Brown, who had been a slave in Georgia, later recalled, "We worked from four in the morning till twelve before we broke our fast, and from that time till eleven or twelve at night." J. W. Terill, a man who spent his slave days in Louisiana and Texas, recalled that on the Texas farm where he worked "the overseer waked us 'bout three in the morning and then he worked us just long as we could see." On President James K. Polk's plantations a day's task was defined "as much work as the meanest full hand can do in nine hours working." Both men and women had to keep up.

Pregnant women and women with small children were not exempted from day or evening work. Women who were far along in their

A page from the log of a plantation hospital in Georgia shows that on February 6, 1839, 39 slaves were treated for a variety of conditions ranging from headaches to childbirth.

pregnancy were assigned to work gangs that did "light hoeing," and if they worked on cotton plantations they were expected to do some picking until well into their pregnancy. When pregnant women got very far advanced they were not allowed to just rest. On the contrary, they spun thread, wove cloth, and made plantation clothing. Women with infants or small children had an especially tiring day. As outlined by former slave Clayborn Gantling, women on the Terrell County, Georgia, plantation of Judge Williams had it hard. "Women with little babies," he reported, "would have to go to work in de mornings with the rest, come back, nurse their children and go back to the field, stay two or three hours, then go back and eat dinner; after dinner dey would have to go to de field and stay two or three more hours and go and nurse the chillun again, go back to the field and stay till night."

Slaves would not have done all of this work if they had not been compelled to do it. Of course, slave masters like to think that slaves were happiest when they were at work. Some even made this claim as part of the pro-slavery argument. But most slaveholders understood that it was the threat of physical punishment that kept slaves hard at their jobs. "It is a pity," wrote a North Carolina planter, "that Slavery and Tyranny must go together and that there is no such thing as having an obedient and useful Slave, without the painful exercise of undue and tyrannical authority." This authority was given to slaveholders by the courts and the state legislatures, which deemed that slaves had to give absolute obedience to their owners. In fact, this was the foundation of the master-slave relationship. A southern judge summed it up best when he said: "The power of the master must be absolute, to render the submission of the slave perfect."

In fact, the submission of most slaves was never perfect, and they could seldom do as much work as fast as the owners demanded. This is one reason why slaves were whipped: to get them to work harder, faster. This was certainly the case on Edwin Eppes's Louisiana plantation, where the end of the cotton-picking day brought fear instead of relief. At sundown the cotton was weighed, and no matter how much cotton they had picked, the slaves carried their cotton to the gin house in fear. As told by kidnapped slave Solomon Northup, "If it falls short in weight—if he has not performed the full task appointed him, he knows that he must suffer. And if he has exceeded it by ten or twenty pounds, in all probability his master will measure the next day's task accordingly. So whether he has too little or too much, his approach to the gin-house is always with fear and trembling. . . .After weighing, follow the whippings."

On antebellum southern plantations whipping and work went hand in hand. For instance, on one Alabama estate, women who had just given birth to infants and were still confined to the slave cabins had to spin thread. According to an ex-slave named Cato, "If they did not spin seven or eight cuts a day they got a whipping." Another former slave remembered that the overseer tied slow workers to a tree at night with nothing to eat. If the slaves did not speed up their work the next day, the overseer "hit [them] thirty-nine licks with a belt, what was 'bout three foot long and four inches wide." Ben Simpson, a Georgia slave, remembered how his master would use a "great, long whip platted out of rawhide" to hit a slave in the gang who would "fall behind or give out."

Overseers' and drivers' reports tell the same gruesome story. These black and white men who worked for slaveholders had the prime responsibility for the production of the crop. White overseers attended to the overall day-to-day and season-to-season strategy of plantation work, and black drivers were on-the-spot disciplinarians who made sure the work got done. Charged with managing slaves to ensure that the plantation turned a profit, and faced with the loss of their position if it did not, both overseer and driver used any means necessary to make slaves work as hard as possible. This was especially true on plantations where the owners were absent. Without the supervision of slaveholders, who were obviously more interested than their managers in protecting their investment in the slaves, overseers and drivers could and often did use as much force as they wanted. This disturbed those who were vigorous supporters of slavery. Pro-slavery southerner Daniel R. Hundley admired and defended the South's institutions. Nevertheless, he admitted that "the overseers on many southern plantations, are cruel and unmercifully severe."

Even those overseers and drivers not considered especially brutal revealed the inherent violence of the system. For instance, in one of his weekly reports Robert Allston's overseer casually noted that he had "flogged for hoeing corn bad Fanny 12 lashes, Sylvia 12, Monday 12, Phoebee 12, Susanna 12, Salina 12, Celia 12, Iris 12." George Skipwith, a black driver for John Hartwell Cocke, a Virginia planter, was equally

A white woman whips a slave. For slaves, violent attacks could come from any direction, and at any time.

Two black slave drivers. Black slave drivers could be just as brutal as their white counterparts.

liberal with the whip. In 1847 he reported to his master that several slaves who worked under him "at a reasonable days work" should have plowed seven acres apiece but had only done one and a half. Therefore, without a thought of the unreasonableness of his demands, and without sympathy for those of his own race, Skipwith reported, "I gave then ten lick a peace upon their skins [and] I gave Julyann eight or ten licks for misplacing her hoe."

That Skipwith was black and that he wielded the whip as readily as any white man should come as no surprise. It was to the slaveholders' advantage to allow blacks a measure of supervision over some of the day-to-day work. Not only could overseers not be everywhere at once, but their tenure on a particular plantation was often short-term. In contrast, as a slave, and a valued one at that, the driver's service was perpetual, and because it was he provided continuity that made for the smooth running of the plantation. Since drivers lived with the slaves, their supervisory role extended into the after-work hours, hours spent away from white overseers. In fact, it was this familiarity with the slaves that made the drivers so necessary. Although it was illegal, some masters never even hired white overseers, but relied on the driver, a man who usually knew as much, if not more, about the daily management of a plantation.

Like overseers, drivers came with all kinds of temperaments and skills. Some were particularly cruel and mean. They raped women and used their power to prey on their fellow bondsmen. Such was the driver remembered by Jane Johnson, a former South Carolina slave. According to her, the driver was "de meanest man, white or black." Other drivers, though, used skillful methods of leadership to get their way. They used the whip only when necessary. They mediated disputes between slaves and acted as their representative to the master. They earned the respect of their fellow slaves and therefore their compliance. Such was the driver remembered by West Turner of Virginia. This driver whipped hard only when the master was looking. At other times "he never would beat dem slaves," but tie them up and pretend to beat them.

However they accomplished their jobs, drivers were part and parcel of the system that not only got maximum work out of the slave but also ensured "perfect submission." Indeed, slaveholders could command a slave's labor only if they could minimize the slave's resistance to their authority. Resistance, no matter how slight, was rightfully perceived as a reflection of independence. Since independence was clearly incompatible with slavery, all behavior on the part of the slave that suggested even a hint of self-determination had to be squelched. Dependence had to be instilled. Slaves who showed too much self-direction were deemed rebellious and judged dangerous. Punishment, therefore, served the purpose of making slaves work, but it also functioned to awe the slave with a sense of the master's power. And power is what the master used to make the slave stand in fear.

The slaveholder and his family demonstrated their power in a variety of ways. To begin with, they always made the slave show deference, not just to them but to all white people. Slaves had to bow in the presence of whites, they had to give way to whites walking in their path, and they were subject to whippings given by white children. When they approached the overseer or the master they had to show humility. On Charles Ball's plantation the slaves, according to one of Ball's former slaves, "were always obliged to approach the door of the mansion, in the most humble and supplicating manner, with our hats in our hands, and the most subdued and beseeching language in our mouths."

Hand in hand with humility went cheerfulness. Slaveholders feared the rebelliousness of slaves who showed dissatisfaction, and therefore did not tolerate sullen or sorrowful moods. Former slave Henry Watson

City of Mobile,
MAYOR'S OFFICE, 1st *April* 185*9*

On the application of *L C Hubbell* to the Mayor of the City of Mobile, *Mary Ann* aged about *30* years, a mulatto female slave, the property of *L C Hubbell* has leave to reside in a house on *Monroe* Street, between *Cedar and Warren* for one year from date.

Mayor.

City Clerk.

Mary Ann, a slave belonging to L. C. Hubbell of Mobile, Alabama, was issued this pass allowing her to live outside her master's home.

noted that "the slaveholder watches every move of the slave, and if he is downcast or sad,—in fact, if they are in any mood but laughing and singing, and manifesting symptoms of perfect content at heart,—they are said to have the devil in them."

The power to make slaves work and to show deference and false happiness was granted to slaveholders by state and city legislatures through statutes called slave codes. Historians debate the protections afforded blacks by slave laws, but it is clear that throughout the South the legal system was designed to protect the interests of white slave owners. Slavery differed as one went from one region of the South to another, from one crop to another, even from one master to another. What gave the system its uniformity, however, was the consistency of social thought on the matter of slaveholder power. Manifested throughout the South in the slave codes, the white South's thinking about slavery left the enslaved no legal means to challenge actions committed against them in violation of the law.

The Louisiana slave code was typical of other state and city codes. The very first provision stated that the slave "owes to his master, and to his family, a respect without bounds, and an absolute obedience." The code defined slaves as property that could be "seized and sold as real estate." Most of the provisions stated what slaves were prohibited from doing. For instance, slaves could not travel without a pass, nor assemble in groups. They were prohibited from buying and selling any kind of goods and they could not carry arms, nor ride horses without the permission of their master. Besides dictating the behavior of blacks, the codes also restricted the actions of whites. Whites could not sell to, or buy anything from, slaves. Whites could not teach slaves to read or write, and a slaveholder could not free a slave without posting a $1,000 bond guaranteeing that the freed slave would leave the state. The code also made death the penalty a slave suffered if he or she willfully harmed the master, mistress, their children, or the overseer. If a slave set fire to the crop or any part of the owner's property, if a slave raped any white female or assaulted any white person in an attempt to escape from slavery, the code also made death the punishment.

Whether or not the slave codes were enforced, the stories told by ex-slaves reveal this system of forced labor to be just as cruel and inhumane as the statutes suggest it was. Even the "kindest" masters kept their slaves illiterate, broke up families through sale, gave them too much work, and fed their slaves a diet that lacked fresh meat, dairy products, and vegetables. Throughout the South slave children were denied proper physical care and emotional support, and adult slaves were stripped naked and whipped in front of family and friends for the slightest infractions. Sadly, too, the presence of thousands of mulatto children gave undeniable testimony to the frequency of the sexual abuse of black women.

And yet, African Americans survived this barbarity better than any enslaved black people in the Western Hemisphere. It was not easy to do because slavery's persistence was based on keeping individual blacks dependent, and the race as a whole weak. Survival was a tribute to the North American slave's ability to adapt and resist, and to create communities that nourished the strength it took to resist some of the most inhumane aspects of the system.

CHAPTER 3
SLAVE COMMUNITIES
◇ ◇ ◇

I n the slave quarters, far removed from the eyes and ears of the
slave master and his family, slave parents told their children the
now-classic story of Br'er Rabbit, the Wolf, and Tar Baby. The
story begins when the strong and powerful Wolf creates a sticky
doll, or Tar Baby, to trap Rabbit, who is inquisitive and sly.
While walking through the woods one day, Rabbit comes upon Tar Baby
sitting by the side of the road, where it has been placed by Wolf. Being a
friendly sort, Rabbit greets it with a "Hello, howdy do." When Tar Baby
does not reply, the angry Rabbit hits the baby doll. First one hand gets
stuck, then the other. Losing his temper even further, Rabbit kicks Tar
Baby and butts it with his head, only to get his entire body stuck to Tar
Baby.

When Wolf arrives to collect Rabbit, he decides to kill him by burning him in the brush. Instead of cringing in fear, Rabbit's clever response
is to pretend that he wants to feel the warmth of fire on his coat. Wolf
falls for Rabbit's deception and decides that the thorny briar patch might
be a more suitable punishment. Rabbit, however, knows that if he gets
thrown in the briar patch he can work his way loose from Tar Baby and
escape. He therefore pretends to cringe at Wolf's threat: "Mercy, mercy,
whatever you do, please don't throw me in the briar patch." Wolf falls for
Rabbit's feigned terror and throws him in the briar patch, whereupon
Rabbit makes a quick escape.

In the assortment of tales told by adult slaves to the young was another about a very talkative slave. In this tale, the slave comes across a

*A burial service con-
ducted by an African-
American preacher
and attended solely by
slave mourners.*

frog who can speak. Amazed at such a wonder, the slave runs and tells his master of this miracle. The master does not believe the slave and threatens to punish him if he is lying. When the frog refuses to talk for the master, the slave is beaten severely. Only when the master leaves does the frog speak, saying, "A tol' yuh 'de othah day, yuh talk too much."

These are only two of the hundreds of tales that were told in the slave quarters, but if we use these tales to represent plantation life, they tell us a great deal about the relationship between slaves and masters. One thing they tell us is that masters did not always have their way. Wolf had Rabbit in his control, at his mercy, but he was still unable to conquer him. Slaves learned from this. They learned that quick-wittedness was an essential survival trait, and that deception could give the weak some control over the strong, allowing the powerless to survive with a minimal amount of physical or emotional assault. The story also laid bare the concepts that might did not always make for right, and that rash behavior, like that indulged in by Rabbit, seldom yielded rewards. These were important lessons for the slave child. They were lessons about life—not a life that was distant and abstract, but one the slave had to live every day.

The same was true of the second story. Though simpler than the first, it taught young blacks important lessons about survival. First, it showed the slave's world to be unpredictable. Where else but in a world filled with uncertainty would a frog speak, and speak to a powerless slave, at that? In the slave's real world, masters, angry at God knows what, might lash out at a slave at any moment. A mistress might all of a sudden find fault with her housemaid and strike out with a fist or a foot. A year or two of bad harvests might lead to a slaveholder's financial ruin, forcing him to sell some of his slaves. This might separate parent from child, husband from wife, brother from sister.

What the slave learned from the story of the talking frog was that the best defense against unpredictability was silence, the key to secrecy. Silence kept masters ignorant of everything that went on behind their backs: the food slaves stole, the religious services held in secret, the escapes made by the boldest of slaves, the anger and hatred that blacks felt toward whites. Silence protected the slave quarters. It kept the slave family and the slave's religious life removed from white invasion. In other words, the story taught the slave child how to protect African-American plantation communities.

Children were given chores at an early age. Here they play in front of their cabins.

If masters could have survived without the slave community they no doubt would have. Work, not community, was what they wanted most from slaves. Relationships that gave the slave points of reference outside of their influence were not as important as those that put the slave under their control. They did not want bonded men and women to have too many roles that were independent of that assigned to them. Therefore, to the master, the fact that African Americans were parents, preachers, or anything other than laborers was immaterial. They demanded, and usually got, obedient workers.

And yet, because masters and slaves were locked in a cycle of mutual dependency that both understood, their demands aided the development of the slave community. Slaves knew that the laws of slavery gave the master the power of life and death; and that these laws in turn made them dependent on their master's good will. But they also knew that as long as slave owners relied on them for their wealth there

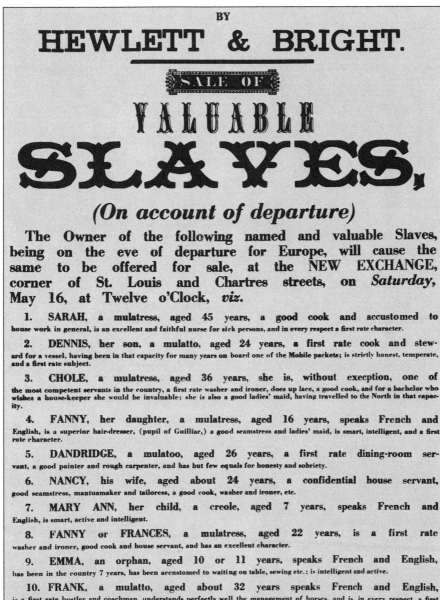

BY
HEWLETT & BRIGHT.

SALE OF

VALUABLE
SLAVES,

(On account of departure)

The Owner of the following named and valuable Slaves, being on the eve of departure for Europe, will cause the same to be offered for sale, at the NEW EXCHANGE, corner of St. Louis and Chartres streets, on *Saturday,* May 16, at Twelve o'Clock, *viz.*

1. SARAH, a mulatress, aged 45 years, a good cook and accustomed to house work in general, is an excellent and faithful nurse for sick persons, and in every respect a first rate character.

2. DENNIS, her son, a mulatto, aged 24 years, a first rate cook and steward for a vessel, having been in that capacity for many years on board one of the Mobile packets; is strictly honest, temperate, and a first rate subject.

3. CHOLE, a mulatress, aged 36 years, she is, without execption, one of the most competent servants in the country, a first rate washer and ironer, does up lace, a good cook, and for a bachelor who wishes a house-keeper she would be invaluable; she is also a good ladies' maid, having travelled to the North in that capacity.

4. FANNY, her daughter, a mulatress, aged 16 years, speaks French and English, is a superior hair-dresser, (pupil of Guilliac,) a good seamstress and ladies' maid, is smart, intelligent, and a first rate character.

5. DANDRIDGE, a mulatoo, aged 26 years, a first rate dining-room servant, a good painter and rough carpenter, and has but few equals for honesty and sobriety.

6. NANCY, his wife, aged about 24 years, a confidential house servant, good seamstress, mantuamaker and tailoress, a good cook, washer and ironer, etc.

7. MARY ANN, her child, a creole, aged 7 years, speaks French and English, is smart, active and intelligent.

8. FANNY or FRANCES, a mulatress, aged 22 years, is a first rate washer and ironer, good cook and house servant, and has an excellent character.

9. EMMA, an orphan, aged 10 or 11 years, speaks French and English, has been in the country 7 years, has been accustomed to waiting on table, sewing etc.; is intelligent and active.

10. FRANK, a mulatto, aged about 32 years speaks French and English, is a first rate hostler and coachman, understands perfectly well the management of horses, and is, in every respect, a first rate character, with the exception that he will occasionally drink, though not an habitual drunkard.

All the above named Slaves are acclimated and excellent subjects; they were purchased by their present vendor many years ago, and will, therefore, be severally warranted against all vices and maladies prescribed by law, save and except FRANK, who is fully guaranteed in every other respect but the one above mentioned.

TERMS:—One-half Cash, and the other half in notes at Six months, drawn and endorsed to the satisfaction of the Vendor, with special mortgage on the Slaves until final payment. The Acts of Sale to be passed before WILLIAM BOSWELL, *Notary Public,* at the expense of the Purchaser.

New-Orleans, May 13, 1835.

PRINTED BY BENJAMIN LEVY.

When the owner of these slaves moved to Europe, he auctioned off his slaves individually. Slave families lived with the constant fear that they could be torn apart or sold away from one another at any moment.

were limits to the slaveholder's power. Masters understood this too. They had the power of life and death over the slave, but dead slaves could not cultivate crops, and injured or rebellious slaves could not work. In the end both master and slave settled on an arrangement that took into account this mutual dependence. Though complex in its workings, the relationship that developed was really quite simple. In general, as long as slaves did their work with diligence, deference, and obedience, masters allowed them some discretion over how they spent their non-work time.

The slave family was at the center of life on the plantation, but was viewed in different ways by the master and his enslaved workers. For the master, slave families provided a means of organizing the plantation. Rather than the barrack-style living that one found in the Caribbean and Latin America, slaves in the American South lived in quarters with their families. These living arrangements made for less rebelliousness among the slaves, a fact that masters took advantage of. As early as the 1770s, the Earl of Egmont, then governor of a colony the British were trying to establish in east Florida, wrote to his overseer and English backers requesting women as companions for the slave men there. Fearing that the men would run away, he wrote that women "would greatly tend to keep them at home and to make them Regular." Many years later a Raleigh, North Carolina, slave confirmed the Earl's observation. When asked by a curious northern traveler why he did not run away, the man said: "I might be sold away from them [his family], which I won't be if I don't try to run away."

Husbands and children had the same effect on slave women. For years the Flint family's hold upon Harriet Brent Jacob's children kept her from fleeing. In her narrative Jacobs explained: "I was certain my children were to be put in their power, in order to give them a stronger hold upon me." Similarly, in 1838 a slave name Clarissa was sent to Philadelphia even though there was some concern about her running away once she reached free territory. What kept Mrs. Trigg, her mistress, from worrying about her escape were Clarissa's husband and children, who remained in Kentucky.

Although slave owners used the slave family to maintain control over bonded men and women, their most obvious use for the family was to reproduce the slave population. This was especially so after the foreign slave trade became illegal in 1807. After that the only legal way for a master to increase his holdings in slaves was to purchase them from another slaveholder or a slave trader, or encourage his own slaves to have children. The latter means was preferred because it was cheaper, easier, and the most natural. Natural because slaves had their own reasons for wanting to have children, and easier because it usually did not require forceful intervention by the master.

Families therefore were in the master's best interest and fertility statistics prove it. In each year between 1800 and the Civil War more than one-fifth of the black women between the ages of 15 and 44 years of age bore a child. On average female slaves had their first child at age 19, two years before the average southern white woman had hers. Slave women continued having children at two-and-a-half-year intervals until they reached the age of 39 or 40. It bears repeating that this level of fertility is what made North American slavery unique in the Western Hemisphere. In most other places slave owners relied heavily on purchasing new slaves from Africa.

To say that slave owners relied heavily on natural increase is not to say that they did not try hard to manipulate family formation. In addition to the verbal prodding to encourage young women to reproduce,

South Carolina planter Charles Cotesworth Pinckney kept detailed inventories of his slaves, listing their age, character, and other pertinent information such as who their parents were and when they were acquired.

slave owners used more subtle techniques as part of the management of their plantations. For example, most, though by no means all, pregnant and nursing women did less work and received more food than non-pregnant women. Frances Kemble reported that on her husband's Georgia and South Carolina rice plantations, when children were born "certain additions of clothing and an additional weekly ration were bestowed upon the family." If inducements such as these were not sufficient to secure the cooperation of the slave of childbearing age, the master always had recourse to punishment. According to ex-slave Berry Clay, "a barren women was separated from her husband and usually sold." And it was not uncommon for slaveholders to demand their money back for female slaves they had purchased who later proved incapable of giving birth.

If the treatment of infertile women like barren sows confirmed the manipulation of slave childbearing, the resort to outright force only added further proof that masters had a financial interest in slave families. The story of a Texan, Rose Williams, is a case in point. According to Williams she had been at Master Hawkins's place for about a year when Hawkins approached her and told her he was changing her housing assignment: "You gwine live with Rufus in that cabin over yonder. Go fix it for living." Rose attributed her unsuspecting attitude to her youth (she was only about 16), for she assumed that she was only "to tend cabin for Rufus." She soon learned that she was actually being forced to accept Rufus as her husband. When she refused to have sexual relations with him, Rufus complained to Hawkins, who told Rose that it was her duty to "bring forth portly children." Reinforcing his point, he told Rose that he had paid "big money" for her "'cause I wants you to raise me childrens." She complied with his wishes under threats of a beating and out of fear that she would be sold away from her family: "I thinks 'bout Massa buying me offen the block and saving me from being separated from my folks and 'bout being whipped at the stake. There it am. What am I's to do?...I yields."

Most slave women were luckier than Rose Williams. In fact, because most slaves wanted a family life they actively sought out their own mates and did what they could to make the family a stable unit. It was hard, of course. The slave master's power was disruptive. But it was the family that softened the impact of that power. The family was the buffer that stood between the master and the individual slave.

Only in the eyes of the law and the master were slave marriages not binding. For slaves who had chosen their own spouses, marriage vows were sacred. It did not matter that the ceremony was often a simple ritual, sometimes accompanied by the act of jumping over a broom to symbolize the beginning of domestic living together. For slaves, it was attended with reverence.

And for good reason. The family gave the slave a point of reference that did not begin and end with the master. It gave bonded men and women the role of parent. It gave their children the sibling role, which evolved into the roles of aunt and uncle. With the family, slaves became providers and protectors for their spouses and their children. If parents were lucky enough to survive into old age without being separated, and usually it was a mother surviving with a daughter, then the mother could count on her daughter's care. Clearly, family life happened within the constraints of slavery, but the little room left by the master's dependence on the slave allowed it to happen nevertheless.

Courtship patterns show how the slave community and the family absorbed so much of the pain and desperation of slavery. For instance, during the week the clothes of field workers were tattered and dirty, but on Sundays slaves wore their best clothing. This made a real difference in their otherwise dreary lives, especially the lives of slave women. On Sundays they wore dresses that had been packed all week in sweet-smelling flowers and herbs, dresses perfumed to attract the opposite sex. Ex-slave Gus Feaster had pleasant remembrances of the women who "took their hair down outen the strings," who charmed the men "wid honeysuckle and rose petals hid in dere bosoms," and who "dried chennyberries and painted dem and wo'em on a string around dere necks."

If courtship allowed for feminine expression it also gave men the opportunity to demonstrate masculinity in a domain not controlled by the master. Men went to great lengths to attract the attention of young women. One Louisiana man named Sam danced an entire Christmas party away trying to impress his sweetheart by proving himself to be the best dancer on the plantation. A Georgia slave named Abraham used a different tactic to get female attention. He "borrowed" his master's boots and horse and went off to a nearby frolic where, as predicted, he "got all the gals attentions."

This plantation scene was painted by an unknown artist sometime between 1790 and 1800. It was originally thought to be a depiction of a wedding ceremony in which slaves jumped over a broomstick, but scholars now believe that it might depict a secular West African dance performed with scarves and sticks.

When these courtship rituals resulted in marriage, the slave could count on an even greater variety of roles, not to mention a new kind of companionship. From each other, slave husbands and wives could count on compassion. Remembering his father, an ex-slave recalled, "My mother just rejoiced in him. Whenever he sat down to talk she just sat and looked and listened."

In what was, by necessity, an egalitarian marital relationship, both parents provided what extras they could for each other, their children, and other family members. As parents, slaves also educated their children. Part of that education included teaching the children how to become good parents and providers when they grew older. Fathers took pride in teaching their sons how to trap wild turkeys and rabbits, how to run down and catch raccoons, how to build canoes out of great oak logs. Mothers taught their daughters how to quilt and sew, and hunt and fish, too. Both parents told their kids the animal stories that taught so many lessons about how to live in a cruel and uncertain world. And usually, at their own peril, both parents did what they could to show their children how to protect their own. A case in point involved the mother of

Fannie Moore. With pride, Moore recalled that in the face of hatred from "de old overseer," her mother stood up for her children and would not let them be beaten. For that "she get more whippin . . . dan anythin' else."

Lest we err on the side of idealism, it should be remembered that for all the good the family could do for the slave it could also be a source of heartbreak and did in fact lessen resistance to the master. Few men who had romantic relationships with women escaped without wounded pride, enduring anger, and a diminished sense of manhood. Louis Hughes stood stark still, blood boiling, as his master choked his wife for talking back to the mistress. His wife was subsequently tied to a joist in a barn and beaten while he stood powerless to do anything for her. The family was also the scene of domestic violence. When Ellen Botts's mother showed up in the kitchen of a sugar plantation with a lump on her head it was because her hot-tempered husband had put it there. And for all that parents could do for their offspring, they could not shield them from the painful realities of perpetual servitude, from the whip, or from the knowledge that whatever instructions they gave them, masters and mistresses had the ultimate authority.

And yet in the slave's view, the family, with all that could go wrong with it, was the most important unit on the plantation. So much so that when family members were separated by sale or death, unrelated members of the slave community filled in as kin. If a child was left motherless or fatherless an aunt or uncle or close friend "adopted" the child and became its mother or father. Older community members became grandparents to children who had none. When men from Upper South slave states like Virginia and North Carolina were sold to the new Lower South states of Mississippi, Alabama, and Arkansas they created brothers and sisters of slaves who, like themselves, had been separated from their real family. Always there was this familial bonding, always the search for an identity that made the slave more than a beast of burden.

The slave's sacred world, reflected in song, music, religion, and folk beliefs, was another space African Americans created apart from the realm of the slave master. Like the family, the sacred world put distance between the master and the slave. It prevented legal slavery from taking over the soul. Even more than the family, which could after all be split apart and affected in other ways by whites, the sacred world, the world that grew from the spirit, inhabited an untouchable sphere.

But as they did with the slave's family, slaveholders tried to control it and use it to their advantage. They especially tried to use religion as a means of social control. "You will find," wrote Thomas Affleck in his instructions to overseers, "that an hour devoted every Sabbath morning to [slaves'] moral and religious instruction would prove a great aid to you in bringing about a better state of things amongst the Negroes." From the slaveholder's point of view a better state of things meant more obedience, less stealing, more hard work. Slave testimony reveals that white preachers always stressed these points. Hannah Scott resented it: "All he say is 'bedience to de white folks, and we hears 'nough of dat without him tellin' us." Maria, Mary Boykin Chesnut's slave, resented it too. She complained bitterly to her South Carolina mistress about a white preacher who, she said, "goes for low life things, hurting people's feel-

A plantation owner and his family attend church services with their slaves. Slaveholders tried to use religion as a tool to more fully dominate the lives of their slaves.

ings." Apparently the preacher's standard text was "Don't you tell lies. Don't you steal!"

The religion the masters ordered for the slave was not only meant to directly control the slave; it was also an attempt to make slavery safer and legitimate. It was no mere coincidence that masters began hiring preachers in great numbers around 1830, the same time that the pro-slavery argument was pushed with greater intensity. Both eased the sometimes troubled mind of the slave master. Religious instruction gave slaveholders the means of imparting their own code of morality, while it also gave them a way to prove to themselves that they were really trying to uplift those they had declared barbaric heathens. The thought that religion could make slavery safer by making slaves less rebellious was an additional source of psychic comfort. For masters who feared that slave ownership dammed their own souls, the religious instruction they gave their slaves was the means by which they hoped to redeem themselves.

Masters made similar use of other aspects of the slave's sacred world. Slave song, for instance, was taken by them and their families as evidence of the slaves' happiness. On some plantations the slave's music even became the centerpiece of entertainment, with blacks asked to perform their spirituals and play their instruments before invited white guests. These performances lent the appearance of master and slave locked in harmonious bliss, each content with their status and rank, each satisfied with their particular "place."

Appearances, though, were deceiving, especially to the master. Slave religion, and the song that was an integral part of it, reflected a world the master could not see. They were the outward manifestation of a worldview possessed by black people. Together with folk beliefs and slave tales, religion and music demonstrated not that slaves were content, nor that slavery was safe. The sacred world of black people demonstrated the indomitable strength of the spirit.

Christianity is a prime example. It was given to slaves one way, but digested another. African Americans took at face value the idea that all men were equal in the sight of God. Because they did they could not take seriously the white preacher's text "slaves obey your masters." "Before God, we are white as he is," said Chesnut's slave in complaining about a white preacher, "and in the pulpit he no need to make us feel we are servants." Almost all African Americans shared Maria's perspective. If God was the all-powerful Master with no one, not even the slave master, above Him, and if all men and women were God's children, without regard to rank and station in life, then all God's children were equal, white and black alike. All, including the slave owner, had to answer to a higher authority.

Slaves believed that the slaveholder, not the slave, was the sinner, and the Bible gave them the evidence that they were right. Hadn't God sent Moses to deliver the Israelites out of bondage? Had he not punished the Egyptians for enslaving his chosen people? Had he not sent his son, Jesus, to redeem the world, and was not Jesus, like the slave, a humble sufferer, a servant? By identifying with the Israelites and with Jesus, the slave turned the master into the sinner and gave himself the inner strength that flowed from the belief in his own salvation in the next world. In his everyday world, this inner strength gave the slave enough psychic freedom to resist becoming completely subservient to white people.

Nowhere was this strength more evident than in the courage slaves revealed in conducting their own religious services, even when they had been forbidden to do so. Said Nancy Williams of Virginia, "Dat ole white preachin' wasn't nothin.' Old white preachers use to talk with dey tongues widdout sayin' nothin'. But Jesus," she said, "told us slaves to talk wid our hearts."

What ex-slave Nancy Williams implied, most slaves believed—that slaves were spiritually superior to whites. This attitude was revealed in their songs. Slaves, not the master, were "de people dat is born of God," "de people of de Lord." When African Americans sang, "I'm a child ob God, wid my soul sot free," they sang of salvation in the afterlife but also of deliverance in this world. Together, away from the master's eyes and ears, black men and women worshipped a God they felt would deliver them the same way he delivered Joshua, Jonah, Moses, and Noah. "O my Lord delivered Daniel," they observed, "O why not deliver me too?"

The deliverance slaves prayed for was not just for the next world. They wanted to be free in this world, and many of the sacred songs contained elements of protest and messages of liberation. For example, when Frederick Douglass, and many of his fellow slaves, sang "O Canaan, sweet Canaan, / I am bound for the land of Canaan," they were singing not only about someday going to heaven, but about reaching the North. The North was also the implied destination in the song "Run to Jesus, shun the danger, / I don't expect to stay much longer here." In the same vein, when slaves sang "Steal Away to Jesus," they were just as likely to be announcing a secret worship service as they were to be talking about salvation. The service, under the direction of preachers African Americans themselves chose, gave slaves a sense of independence, a kind of freedom, and the courage to resist and escape slavery altogether.

Folk beliefs, another crucial part of the slaves' sacred world, also instilled this sense of freedom and resistance. Although most whites, and some slaves, generally found beliefs in fortune tellers, witches, magic signs, and conjurers to be at odds with Christianity, for most slaves there was no gap between the two. The same slave who believed fervently in Jesus Christ could also believe that the dead returned to the living in spiritual visitations, that children born with teeth or as twins came under an ominous sign, that conjuring caused insanity and other illness.

In slave folk religion signs were important. A screech owl's cry was a sign of death that could be countered by turning shoes upside down at a door, or turning one's pockets inside out; a black cat crossing one's path was bad luck unless one spit on the spot where the paths met. Many slaves believed that a cross-eyed person could bring on a spell unless one crossed one's fingers and spat on them.

Dreams were also taken seriously. A former South Carolina slave reported that he dreamed he saw his three uncles skinning a cow and

> A Bill for the better regulation of the con
> =duct of negroes, slaves, and free person
> of colour —
> Be it enacted by the General Assembly of
> the State of North Carolina, and it is hereby
> enacted by the authority of the same; that
> it shall not be lawful under any pretence
> for any free negro, slave, or free person of
> colour to preach or exhort, or in any man-
> =ner to officiate as a preacher, and if any
> free negro, or free person of colour shall be
> thereof duly convicted on indictment before
> any court having jurisdiction thereof
> he shall for each offence receive not
> exceeding thirty nine lashes on his bare
> back, and when any slave shall be
> guilty of a violation of this act, he shall
> on conviction before a single Magistrate
> receive not exceeding thirty nine lashes on
> his bare back —

In 1832, the North Carolina legislature passed this law forbidding blacks to preach.

cutting it open while women and children sat around crying. When he told his mother about the dream she told him that fresh meat in a dream was a sign of death. "Sure enough that very evening Uncle Peter Price died." According to the former slave, his dreams came true so often that the older people on his plantation used his dreams as a way of predicting the future.

And in a way predicting was what folk beliefs were all about. Slaves lived in a world over which they had little control. For them, life held so many uncertainties, so little that was predictable. Folk beliefs provided a way of imposing order on an unstable environment. Like Christianity, slave folk beliefs could not be controlled by whites and therefore became another source of strength.

Although all slaves could make use of this power, conjurers were the people believed to have a special gift for reading signs and dreams, at effecting change through the use of spells, herb mixtures, and charms. African in origin, conjuring survived white attempts to eliminate it. Most slaves feared conjurers as much as they feared the master because they believed that these men and women could bring about all manner of bad or good luck. They could make mean masters kind and kind masters mean, prevent or cause whippings, separations, illness or death, ensure love and happiness or friction and hate. They were especially known for the evil they could do. Rossana Frazier, for instance, blamed a conjurer for her blindness, whereas Nicey Kinney of Georgia thought that "some old witch man conjured me into marrying Jordan Jackson."

Even masters expressed concern over the conjurers' influence. Slaves were known to believe themselves invulnerable when carrying a conjurer's charm. In 1842 the Reverend Charles C. Jones wrote that slaves "have . . . been made to believe that they were under a protection that rendered them *invincible*. That they might go any where and do anything they pleased, and it would be impossible for them to be discovered or known."

Rather than submit to the cures of white medical doctors brought in by masters, African Americans usually preferred to treat their own illnesses and make their own medicines. They had good reason. Since early 19th-century medicine was hardly an exact science, the medical practitioners' treatment was likely to be as successful as that applied by black root and herb doctors. Moreover, like Josephine Bacchus, a South Carolina ex-slave, most slaves distrusted medical doctors. "De people never didn' put much faith in de doctors in dem days," she recalled, "mostly, dey would use de herbs in de fields for dey medicine."

Along with conjurers, slaves put their faith in their own midwives and "doctor women." Any number of broths, made from the leaves and barks of trees, from the branches and twigs of bushes, from turpentine, catnip, or tobacco were used to treat whooping cough, diarrhea, toothaches, colds, fevers, headaches, and backaches. Although they treated both men and women, these particular "healers" specialized in the treatment of women and children. Menstrual cramps, for example, were sometimes treated with a tea made from the bark of the gum tree, and at least one "doctor woman" treated colic by giving the fretting infant a syrup made from a boiled rat's vein. If the effectiveness of this last treatment seems questionable, so too did the midwife's folk practice of putting an axe under the delivery mattress to "cut the pain" of childbirth. The point, however, is not how effective these treatments were; the 19th-century medical practice of bleeding a patient proved just as ineffective a cure as did slave practices. The important consideration is that slaves looked to their own when they were sick or in need of spiritual guidance. Because they did they strengthened their own

A plantation preacher. Slaves were much more likely to listen and respond to a preacher when they were out of the presence of their masters.

community and gave men and women a chance to gain status in their own group.

Indeed, the slave community itself was important. Without their community to confirm and reinforce their families, religion, and folk beliefs, the individual slaves would have had only the master's definition of their existence. With no others to sing with, dance with, or tell stories to, the slave would have been reduced to childlike dependence on the master, who would have put slave customs and familial needs to his use only. As it was, slave children did learn at an early age that they were among the world's weak and powerless. But through the slave tales they learned how to survive and circumvent the powerful. They belonged to a community that, though powerless, put psychological space between themselves and the whites around them.

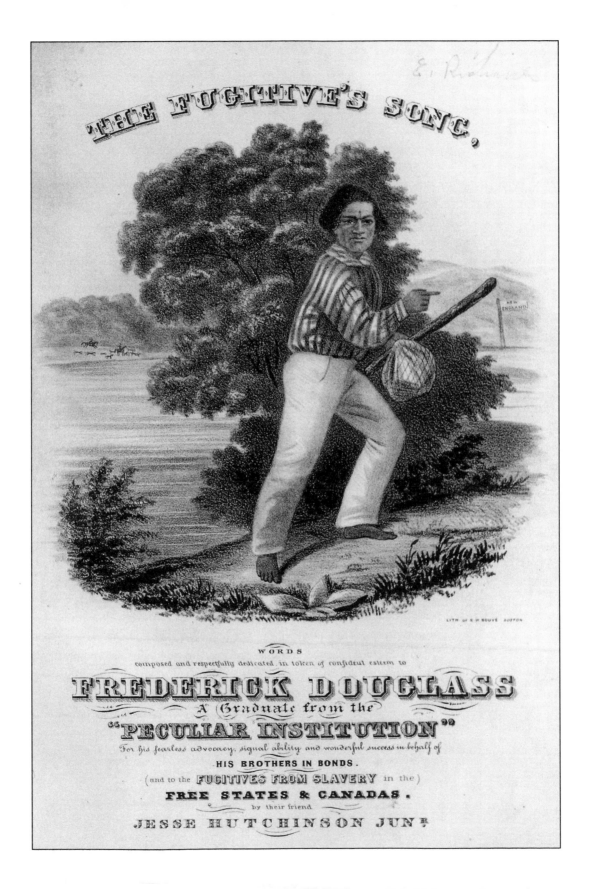

CHAPTER 4

FIT FOR FREEDOM

◇ ◇ ◇

Sometime around 1833, Frederick Douglass looked out across the Chesapeake Bay with his mind bent on freedom. He asked himself, "O why was I born a man, of whom to make a brute!" The more he thought, the more he knew he wanted his freedom:

Why am I a slave? I will run away. I will not stand it. Get caught or get clear. I'll try it. . . . I have only one life to lose. I had as well be killed running as die standing. . . . It cannot be that I shall live and die a slave."

For all the millions of slaves who at one time or another had these thoughts, only about a thousand a year actually acted on them. This is because escape was incredibly difficult. Slaves like Douglass, who were in the Upper South, close to free states, stood the best chance of success. Those close to southern cities also had a good chance, for if they escaped to an urban area they could become lost in its hustle and bustle, as well as in its free-black community. Slaves who accompanied their masters and mistresses on northern trips were also likely runaways, but like any slave they had to have the will to run. This will had to be more powerful than the fear of a brutal whipping or sale away from family and loved ones, more powerful even than the fear of death.

Douglass found he had the needed will when one day he refused to be whipped. His master had hired him out for a year to a man named Edward Covey, who was widely known for his ability to break the spirit of unruly slaves. Covey had almost succeeded in working and beating Douglass into the most abject obedience when Douglass by chance

The Fugitive's Song was composed in 1845 as a tribute to Frederick Douglass, who escaped from slavery in 1833.

57

visited a conjurer, who gave him a root reputed to prevent whippings. As he was told to do, Douglass kept the root in his right pocket. The next time Covey tried to beat him he seized Covey around the throat, flung him to the ground, declared that he would no longer be treated as a brute, and fought off the other slaves Covey got to assist him. The fight continued for two hours, but in the end Douglass won out over Covey, and he was never again whipped by him or any other white man.

The victory Douglass won over Covey was small compared to the one he had won over his own fear. As he put it, "I felt as I never felt before. . . . My long crushed spirit rose, cowardice departed, bold defiance took its place; and I now resolved that, however long I might remain a slave in form, the day had passed forever when I could be a slave in fact." Four years later Douglass escaped from slavery and found his way to New York.

But the records of slavery show that few fled slavery as Douglass did. Fewer still participated in large-scale rebellions aimed at overthrowing the institution. There were, however, many slaves who took a stand against their servitude, who somehow managed to be slaves in form but

A group of slaves escaping from the eastern shore of Maryland. If captured, escaped slaves faced severe physical punishment when returned to their masters.

not in fact. These were men and women who resisted the worst aspects of slavery. Some, like Douglass, refused to be whipped; some ran away for short periods of time. Some feigned ignorance of how to do a particular chore and others feigned illness rather than work to the limits that the master wanted. Still others used individual acts of violence to counter the authority of the master.

Unlike running away, this kind of resistance only separated the slave from the worst aspects of slavery. Its end was not liberty, just release from some of slavery's misery. However, like the slave family, slave Christianity, and folk religion, it nevertheless helped African Americans survive this most inhuman institution. Resistance of all types proved that black people were fit for freedom.

Whatever other circumstance came together in the life of a slave to make him or her commit an act of individual resistance, one thing is for sure: the slave who resisted did not stand in perpetual abject fear of their master, nor did the slave completely lose those qualities which made him or her a whole human being. Slaves who stole extra food, for example, cared enough about their own well-being to defy the slaveholders' rationing system. Slaves who risked their lives in their struggle not to be whipped were making a personal statement about their self-esteem and individual honor. Women who kicked and clawed their sexual abusers made eloquent statements about their personal dignity. These individual acts of resistance were attempts to retain or take back some control over lives that were by law assigned to someone else.

Nowhere is this more apparent than the attempts by some slaves to get enough to eat. The usual fare on most farms and plantations from Virginia to Mississippi was salt pork and corn meal. When they could, slaves supplemented this with vegetables grown in their own gardens, and meat and fish they caught. Most slaves needed more and most stole what they needed. Many did not view stealing from the master as something sinful. Whether they stole clothing, money, crops, or food, slaves often justified their actions with the argument that not only had they worked for the goods, but they were simply moving them from one part of the master's property to another.

This thinking was especially obvious during the Civil War. Those who fled to Union troops taking their master's goods with them felt that the promised time of retribution had arrived. Southern mistress Adele Pettigru Allston probably made an accurate assessment of the slave's attitude when she complained: "The conduct of the negroes in robbing our house, store room, meat house, etc., and refusing to restore anything shows you they *think it right* to steal from us, to spoil us, as the Israelites did the Egyptians."

Many slaves did not wait until the Civil War to act this way. Besides stealing, they burned gin houses, barns, corncribs, and smokehouses. Some slaves used poison or outright physical force to kill their masters. Capture always meant certain death, but they did it nonetheless.

To guard against violence, especially that which could lead to large-scale rebellions, slaveholders created the slave patrols. These were groups of white males, usually of the lower classes, called together to look for runaways, to prevent slave gatherings, and generally ensure the safety of the white community. Since slaves were not allowed to travel the countryside without a pass from their master, a principal task of the patrols was to enforce the pass system. This they often did with excessive brutality, administering beatings on the authority given them by slaveholders who used the patrol system as a way of binding all whites together against all blacks.

Despite the patrol system slaves resisted. They used passes written by the few in their own group who could read and write. They sheltered runaways in their cabins, and they laid traps that tripped up patrollers' horses.

Some slaves just stood and fought. Like the young Frederick Douglass, they decided that they would not be whipped—not by their master, not by the overseer, and not by a patroller. When Lucy, an Arkansas slave made such a decision, it was because she did not want to be beaten by an overseer. According to her son, "She jumped on him and like to tore him up." Her decision was made at the pain of sale. For such self-assertion others were sold, or worse yet, killed. Some though, like Douglass, managed to stand their ground and avoid retribution and the whip.

Also like Douglass, some found the courage to escape, and many more found the will to try. Georgia slave John Brown ran away several times before he finally succeeded. One time he got as far as Tennessee; another time, thinking he was going north, he traveled almost all of the way on foot to New Orleans. Each time he was captured he was whipped, chained, and had bells attached to him. Over and over again he escaped until he finally reached Indiana. Aunt Cheyney of the Kilpatrick cotton

Plantation police checking the passes of slaves on a road near New Orleans.

plantation in Mississippi was not so fortunate, however. One of her master's mistresses, she had recently given birth to the fourth of her master's children when she ran away. Kilpatrick set his dogs on her trail. When they caught up with her he ordered them to attack. According to her friend Mary Reynolds, "The dogs tore her naked and et the breasts plumb off her body." This served as a punishment for Cheyney, but it was also Kilpatrick's way of warning all slaves, especially women, against running away.

However much African Americans were haunted by these kinds of horrors, there were still those who would not be stopped. The stories of escape reveal as much relentless perseverance as they do ingenuity. Henry "Box" Brown, for example, was carried for 27 hours from Richmond to Philadelphia by Adams Express in a box three feet long and two feet deep. He literally mailed himself to freedom. The light-skinned Ellen Craft escaped by pretending to be a sickly white man traveling in the company of his slave. The slave in attendance was in fact her darker-skinned husband William. Together the two traveled by stagecoach, boat, and train from Georgia to Philadelphia. They stopped at some of the best hotels along the way, and Ellen even conversed with slaveholders about the trouble of runaway slaves.

The person who seemed to give the South the most runaway trouble, though, was Harriet Tubman. She was born a slave some time around 1821 on Maryland's Eastern Shore and lived in slavery for 28 years. Like most slaves in this Upper South region, Tubman lived in dread of being sold to the Deep South. In 1849, when she learned that she was indeed going to be sold, she joined the thousands of others who took to the woods and stole themselves.

What made her unique is that she returned, not once but many times, to rescue others, including her sister, her sister's two children, and her parents. Given the identification of African Americans with the Israelites it should come as no surprise that Tubman was called "Moses." And given the way African Americans used their religion to speak about freedom, it is also not surprising that when Tubman said, "Tell my brothers to be always *watching unto prayer*, and *when the good ship Zion comes along, to be ready to step on board*," this was her signal to leave, not for heaven, but for freedom. It is said that she returned 19 times and rescued more than 300 slaves. She was so good at what she did that Maryland planters offered a $40,000 bounty for her capture.

Henry "Box" Brown mailed himself out of slavery in Richmond, Virginia, to freedom in Philadelphia.

Harriet Tubman, far left, escaped from slavery in 1849 and went on to lead hundreds of other slaves to freedom as a conductor on the Underground Railroad.

Slaveholders wanted to catch Tubman about as much as they wanted to put an end to the Underground Railroad. This network of hiding places run by opponents of slavery provided the slaves fortunate enough to use it with food, shelter, money, clothing, and disguises. A black man, William Still, an officer of the Philadelphia Vigilance Committee, was the moving force behind the Underground Railroad. He wrote of Harriet Tubman that she was "a woman of no pretensions," and "in point of courage, shrewdness, and disinterested exertions to rescue her fellowman, she was without equal."

Indeed, Tubman was unique among all slaves, especially women. This was something William Still knew. Writing about female runaways he observed that "females undertook three times the risk of failure that males are liable to." William Penn, another worker for the Underground Railroad made a similar observation. Speaking of two female runaways, both of whom had two children, he noted: "None of these can walk so far or so fast as scores of *men* that are constantly leaving." The observations of Still and Penn are reflected in statistics on runaways. Men, much more than women, swelled their ranks.

One of the reasons that women had a harder time than men was that they were more reluctant to leave without their children. At the same time, it was the fear of losing them that often provided the incen-

tive to flee. Escaping alone was difficult enough; escaping with children was close to impossible.

There is no question that male runaways regretted leaving their wives and children behind, but women, it seems, suffered a special agony when faced with such a decision. Harriet Brent Jacobs, for instance, was sure that her mistress's vengeance would put her son and daughter in danger of severe punishment, even sale. The advice she sought and was given served only to confuse her and increase her anxiety. From her friend and accomplice, Betty, she received encouragement to escape: "Lors, chile! What's you crying 'bout? Dem young uns vil kill you dead. Don't be so chick'n hearted! If you does, you vil nebber git thro' dis world." But, her grandmother, who, unlike childless Betty, had helped raise three generations of black children, admonished: "Stand by your children, and suffer with them till death. Nobody respects a mother who forsakes her children; and if you leave them, you will never have a happy moment." Jacobs was one of the lucky few. She escaped, and years later so did her son and daughter.

Truancy seems to have been the way many slave women reconciled

This engraving from an 1822 anti-slavery tract shows a black woman and child being kidnapped from their room and taken into slavery.

64

their desire to flee with their need to stay. Men too practiced truancy, but women made the most likely truants because they nursed and were directly responsible for their children. Former slave Benjamin Johnson remembered that sometimes when women would not take a whipping they "would run away an' hide in de woods. Sometimes dey would come back after a short stay an' den dey would have to put de hounds on dere trail to bring dem back home."

Women's short-term flight was by no means a reflection of their lesser courage or greater accommodation to slavery. Truants faced punishment when they returned, punishment many braved over and over again. Moreover, truancy involved as much danger as running away. As Johnson's comment indicates, dogs hunted them down, and the woods and swamps they hid in held all kinds of dangers.

Rather than reflecting a lesser danger, or level of courage, what truancy mirrored was the different slave experiences of men and women, and therefore their different ways of resisting. For example, the division of labor on most farms and plantations conferred greater mobility on males than on female slaves. Few of the chores performed by female slaves took them off the plantation. Usually masters chose their male slaves to assist in the transportation of crops to market, and the transport of supplies and other materials to the plantation. More male than female slaves were artisans and craftsmen, and this made it more difficult to hire out a female slave than a male slave. Fewer female slaves therefore had a chance to vary their work experience. As a consequence, more men than women were able to test their survival skills under different circumstances.

Another factor affecting slave mobility was the "abroad marriage," a union between slaves who resided at different locations. When "abroad" spouses visited each other, usually once a week, it was most often the husband who traveled to the wife. All in all, it was female bondage, more than male bondage, that meant being tied to the immediate environment of the plantation or farm. For these reasons, female slaves much more than male slaves just "stayed put."

This did not mean that they did not resist enslavement or sexual exploitation. Lucy, the woman who would not be whipped, was not the only woman to act that way. There were many, many more. Nor did women always submit to sexual abuse. When Jermain Loguen's mother was attacked she picked up a stick and dealt her would-be rapist a blow that sent him staggering. She stood her ground even as he rebounded with a knife, and finally she knocked him out cold.

By and large though, women did resist in more subtle ways. For instance, they "played the fool" more than men. In other words, in order to avoid doing some onerous chore, they would smile humbly and pretend to misunderstand instructions given by the master, mistress, or overseer. The use of poison also suited women because they officiated as cooks and nurses on the plantation. As early as 1755 a Charleston slave woman was burned at the stake for poisoning her master, and in 1769 a special issue of the *South Carolina Gazette* carried the story of a slave woman who had poisoned her master's infant child. Since the slave's objective was not to get caught we will never really know just how many whites were ushered by slave women to an early grave.

We also will never know how many instances of illness were actually ruses to escape backbreaking labor. Women had an advantage over men in this realm because childbearing was a primary expectation that slave owners had of slave women. In an age where women's diseases were still shrouded in mystery, getting the maximum amount of work from women of childbearing age while remaining confident that no damage was done to their reproductive organs was a guessing game that few white slave owners wanted to play or could afford to lose. In deference to their "mysterious" conditions, women, especially those of childbearing age, were seldom designated as able-bodied workers. Unlike healthy young and middle-aged men who were considered full hands, women, depending on their stage of pregnancy and their frequency of nursing, were labeled three-quarter hands, half hands or quarter hands. Men could and did feign illness. But since women did, in fact, have more sickness because of menstruation and childbirth, they were more likely to get away with it.

Whether they also got away with birth control and abortion is something we will never know. Few 19th-century women, white or black, were ignorant of the ways and means of avoiding pregnancy. The decline in the birth rate among white Americans from 7.04 in 1800 to 3.56 by the eve of the 20th century is evidence of the use of birth control, including abortion. For white women, particularly those of the urban middle classes, a small family had its benefits, not the least of which was the lower risk of dying in childbirth and the ability to spend more time with an individual child.

The cover of The Anti-Slavery Record *for September 1835 shows a mother about to murder her children to save them from the horrors of life as slaves. Though infrequent, infanticide did occur.*

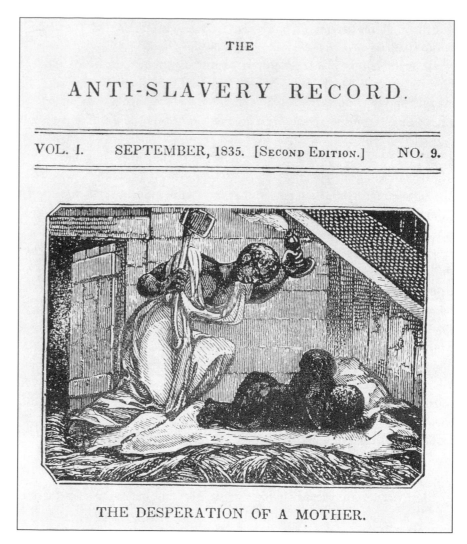

THE
ANTI-SLAVERY RECORD.

VOL. I.   SEPTEMBER, 1835. [Second Edition.]   NO. 9.

THE DESPERATION OF A MOTHER.

The slave woman, however, had no such benefit. In fact, though she, like other 19th-century women, approached pregnancy with fear and never had enough time to spend with any of her children, she risked sale if she remained childless. The risk notwithstanding, some women just refused to have children. How they managed to stay childless, what methods of birth control they used, and the frequency of abortion, remained secrets that were virtually exclusive to the female world of the slave quarters.

Though few slave women divulged these secrets, slaveholders were convinced that black women knew how to avoid pregnancy and also how to bring on a miscarriage. A Tennessee physician, Dr. John H. Morgan, wrote that slave women used the herbs of tansy and rue, the roots and seeds of the cotton plant, cedar berries, and camphor to bring about miscarriage, and Dr. E. M. Pendleton claimed that planters regularly complained of whole families of women who fail to have any children.

More serious were the infrequent cases of infanticide. Women who chose to kill children they had risked their life having were clearly desperate. Yet they struck out at the system where they knew it would hurt, where they knew they had real impact—in the increase of the slave population. That they hurt themselves more than they hurt the master can be assumed, for they were either prosecuted and hanged, or they suffered emotional distress forever.

And yet it was grief and a feeling of being trapped that led them to the desperate act. Thus an Alabama woman killed her child to save it from the mistress's abuse. She claimed that the master was the baby's father, and that her mistress knew it, and treated the infant so cruelly that she had to kill the baby to save it from further suffering. Another woman killed her newborn because she knew that her Texas master had plans to sell the baby, the same way he had sold her three older children. Years later, Lou Smith, her friend recalled the incident: "When her fourth baby was born and was about two months old, she just studied all the time about how she would have to give it up, and one day she said, 'I just decided I'm not going to let Old Master sell this baby: he just ain't going to do it.' She got up and give it something out of a bottle, and pretty soon it was dead."

If African Americans could have overthrown the system that forced such tragic decisions, they would have. But black people faced hopeless odds. Unlike other slaves in other nations in the Americas, black people in the United States were overwhelmingly outnumbered by whites and grouped in small numbers on plantations that were miles apart. Whites had the guns, the ammunition, the horses, the dogs, and the law. They had the resources to crush any revolt by slaves, and the slaves knew it. Resistance, therefore, was individual because it had to be; whites put down the few large-scale rebellions and planned revolts with a viciousness that served notice that revolt was futile.

In spite of the odds and the repression, rebellions did occur, and conspiracies abounded. Among the first was the largest—an uprising in 1811 of close to 400 slaves in St. Charles and St. John the Baptist par-

In Florida and elsewhere in the South, blacks joined with Seminoles in their fight against whites.

ishes in Louisiana. Led by a slave named Charles Deslondes, the slaves sent whites fleeing their plantations for safety in New Orleans. Further east, in 1817 and 1818 blacks joined the Seminole Indians in their fight to keep their Florida homelands. To defend themselves, units of blacks and Indians raided plantations in Georgia, killing whites and carrying off slaves. Again in 1835 blacks joined the Seminoles in their unsuccessful fight against the militias of Florida, Georgia, and Tennessee. Seminole lands had continued to be havens for runaway slaves, and by the 1830s President Andrew Jackson was determined to eliminate these independent communities and seize all Indian lands for white slaveholders. By

that time, though, it was hard to call Seminole land Indian territory because blacks and Indians had intermarried to the extent that they were
indistinguishable. Indeed, so many hundreds of blacks fought on the side
of the Seminoles that United States general Thomas Jesup declared:
"This, you may be assured, is a negro, not an Indian war."

General Jesup understood what all slaveholders knew—that resistance had always gone hand in hand with slavery. The century had begun
with Gabriel Prosser's attempt to seize Richmond, and the year he died,
1800, was the year that Denmark Vesey bought his freedom from his
master and began his life as a free man. That same year Nat Turner was
born. Both men were to become the slaveholder's worst nightmare.

Vesey was a free African-American carpenter who worked hard
enough to become not just self-supporting but relatively wealthy by the
standards of the day. He was a proud, literate, free black man who hated
slavery and hated to see his people bowing and scraping to whites. At age
53 he gathered around him trusted black men, both free and slave, and
planned to capture the city of Charleston. His followers were church
leaders and craftsmen. One of them, Gullah Jack, was a conjurer. For
months they planned their attack on the arsenal at Charleston and on
plantations surrounding the city. During this time they recruited slaves and
free men who had the steady nerves to carry out the plan. Then, on a fateful
day in 1822, they were betrayed. Betrayal meant capture, and capture meant

*This depiction of scenes
from the Nat Turner
rebellion appeared
in an anti-abolitionist
tract in 1831. The
numbers identify
various incidents that
took place during the
rebellion.*

death. Peter Poyas, one of Vesey's lieutenants, went to the galleys with the words of the spirituals on his lips. "Fear not," he told the blacks of Charleston, "the Lord God that delivered Daniel is able to deliver us."

Nat Turner believed himself to be the deliverer. He carried himself in the manner of a messiah. Proud and self-confident, literate and articulate, he saw visions of God's deliverance of black people from bondage. He felt himself to be the Moses who would lead his people out of bondage. Acting on that feeling, Turner led about 70 slaves in an assault on the whites of Southampton, Virginia. In one of the most clear-cut cases of slave rebellion that occurred in this country, Nat Turner went from one plantation to the next killing whites. His instructions to his fellow insurrectionists were followed to the letter. They spared no one. Age and sex made no difference.

In the end Nat Turner was caught. By the time his murder count reached around 60, bands of white men caught up with his men and put down the revolt. Turner took to the woods and managed to evade capture until most of his men had been put to death. As had happened in the Prosser and Vesey conspiracies, the fear of insurrection spread across the South with alarming speed, and whites lashed out mercilessly at blacks, especially those in the vicinity of the rebellion. Anyone suspected of aiding Turner was put to death. All acts of disrespect were taken as a direct challenge to white authority, and slaves who did not act in the most humble manner were punished severely, even killed. Blacks were not allowed to hold religious services or gather in groups at all. All blacks, slave and free, were watched by patrols who had their numbers increased and firearms ready. The message was clear. America was home to the free and the brave, but only for those who were white.

Somewhere though, deep down, slaveholders understood that as long as slavery existed so too would resistance. This is one of the reasons why 19th-century slaveholders tried to improve the material conditions of the slaves. They thought that more food, better living quarters, and fewer whippings would make slaves less rebellious and more content and willing to bear all of slavery's burdens.

African Americans did bear slavery's burdens, but not without resistance. The continuing struggle against slavery created the psychic space black people needed to survive, and it proved to contemporary and future generations that though enslaved, African Americans were fit for freedom.

UNITED STATES OF AMERICA,

STATE OF ILLINOIS, *Madison County,* } ss. { To all to whom these Presents may come—GREETING:

Know Ye, That *Mary Jane Long wife of John Long* a person of Color, about _twenty four_ years of age, *five* feet _Three & ½_ inches high, _Mulatto_ _____ complexion, *has two small pitts on each side of her fore head Daughter of Elijah & Dicey Richardson* _____

has exhibited, presented and filed, in the Office of the Clerk of the Circuit Court of the County and State aforesaid, a **CERTIFICATE,** duly authen= ticated, of **FREEDOM,** as such person of Color.

Now, therefore, I, **WM. TYLER BROWN,** Clerk of the Circuit Court of Madison County, State of Illinois, **CERTIFY,** That said _Mary Jane Long_ _____ is a **FREE PERSON OF COLOR,** a resi= dent or citizen of the State of Illinois, and entitled to be respected accord= ingly, in Person and Property, at all times and places, in the due prosecu= tion of _her_ Lawful concerns.

In Testimony whereof, I have, to these Presents, signed my name, and affixed the Seal of said Court, at Edwardsville, this **28th** day of *November* in the year of our Lord one thousand eight hundred and *forty=four*

Wm T Brown   Clerk.

CHAPTER 5

A DIFFERENT KIND OF FREEDOM

◇ ◇ ◇

O n April 8, 1816, April Ellison, a mulatto expert cotton gin-maker, stood with his white master, William Ellison, before a magistrate and five freeholders of the Fairfield District of South Carolina. It was a solemn occasion. No doubt every word, every movement became indelibly etched in April's mind, because it was the day of his manumission, the day that he bought himself out of slavery. At that time, April was 26 years old. By the time he was 30 he had legally changed his name to William, had bought his wife, Matilda, and his daughter, Eliza Ann, out of slavery, and had freed them. He had moved out of the district of his slave youth and established himself as a free person of color in Stateburg, in the Sumpter District. And he had bought two adult male slaves to help him in his business. Two years later, in 1822, he bought an acre of land, and two years after this he petitioned and received permission from the white members of Holy Cross Episcopal Church to worship with them on the main floor of the vestry, away from the slaves and free blacks who were confined to the balcony.

Elizabeth Hobbs, an attractive mulatto, was born into slavery in 1818, a year after Frederick Douglass's birth. She was born in Virginia, but in her teenage years she was sold further south to a North Carolina master by whom she had a son. Repurchased by a member of the family that had sold her to begin with, she was taken to St. Louis, Missouri, where she met and married a black man named James Keckley. Though

A certificate granted to a free black woman to certify her claim to freedom. Free blacks always had to keep such documents close by to avoid being sold into slavery by unscrupulous slave traders.

Although she never learned to read or write, Sojourner Truth spoke eloquently against slavery and for women's rights.

Keckley told her that he was free, he was in fact a slave, and their life together was a short one. Far more long-term in its consequences were Elizabeth Keckley's abilities as a seamstress, skills perfected at her mother's instruction when she was just a child. As a dressmaker in St. Louis, she was so good, and so popular, that her customers offered to lend her the money to buy herself and her son out of slavery. In 1855, when she was 37 years old, Keckley and her son became free persons of color. After she learned to read and write and paid off her loan, she returned east, first to Baltimore, Maryland, then to Washington, D.C. In Washington, her clients were among the city's elite, the most notable being President Lincoln's wife, Mary Todd, to whom she became a companion and friend.

While Keckley was keeping the company of the First Lady, Sojourner Truth was aiding and nursing refugee slaves fleeing the carnage of the Civil War. At the war's beginning she was 61 years old and had in her lifetime been a housekeeper, a preacher, an abolitionist, and a public speaker for women's rights. A dark-skinned woman, she had been born Isabella Bomefree about 1799, and was freed in 1827 by New York State law. Unlike Keckley or Ellison, Truth never learned to read or write, nor did the South ever hold her as a slave. Nonetheless she was eloquent in her attacks against slavery, and more than anyone else of her time, she was steadfast in her public defense of black women.

The lives of William Ellison, Elizabeth Keckley, and Sojourner Truth tell us a lot about the lives of all blacks who were free during the time of slavery. What these three free blacks did and did not do, where and how they could and did live, the opportunities that were open or closed to them serve as guideposts for this discussion of black freedom. More than anything else, their lives, and those of all free African Americans, reveal that black freedom and white freedom were always very different.

The reason for the different realities of black and white freedom was white prejudice. It was strong in the South, where 90 percent of all blacks were slaves and a dark skin was a presumption of bondage. It was equally strong in the North and West where there was an abiding sentiment against both blacks and slavery. What Fanny Kemble, a well-traveled white woman, said of free blacks in the North held true all over the country. "They are not slaves indeed, but they are pariahs, debarred from every fellowship save with their own despised race. . . . All hands are extended to thrust them out, all fingers point at their dusky skin, all tongues . . . have learned to turn the very name of their race into an insult and a reproach."

That some African Americans had a heritage of freedom that predated the American Revolution was of far less significance to whites than

State of North Carolina,

PITT COUNTY.

Before me, G. A. Dancy, Clerk of the Court of Pleas and Quarter Sessions for said County, personally appeared Edmund Robbin and Harriett Gorham residents of said County, lately slaves, but now emancipated, and acknowledged that they do cohabit together as man and wife, and that said cohabitation commenced the .... day of February 1852

G. A. Dancy, C. C. C.

July 2d 1846

This marriage certificate was issued to a free black couple in North Carolina. Legal marriage was one advantage the free black had over the slave.

the fact that they were black. As the 19th century progressed and the country moved closer and closer to the Civil War, a dark skin carried the presumption of slavery in both the North and the South. More and more, free blacks had to prove that they were not slaves. This was a burden that no white person carried, because white skin color carried with it the presumption of freedom.

More than any other freedom struggle, the American Revolution laid the foundation for the free-black population. Not only did most Northern states pass emancipation laws, such as the one that gave Sojourner Truth her freedom, but the chaos created by the revolution allowed thousands of slaves to escape. Adding to these numbers were those who were emancipated as a result of their military service during the war, those whose Southern masters freed them because they felt guilty about holding slaves, and those who were freed because slavery became unprofitable. The result was a free-black population that numbered 59,000 in 1790 and grew to 488,000 by the eve of the Civil War. These numbers were increased by blacks born of free mothers, including those of white women with black partners, and free mulatto immigrants from the West Indies, especially those who fled Haiti after the 1790 slave revolt led by Toussaint L'Ouverture. Every year natural increase added to their numbers.

If it was not the first thing newly freed blacks did, then one of the first actions they took was to change their names. Significantly, they chose English, not African names. In this they confirmed their identity as Westerners and their homeland as America. Their new names also separated them from their slave past. April Ellison provides a good example. The name April, like the names Sambo, Cato, and Pompey, was a name given to blacks by whites. Sometimes designating either a day or month, the names chosen by whites seldom reflected the personal choice of black relatives, and were, like the names Cato and Pompey, sometimes given in ridicule.

Freed African Americans shed their slave names in favor of names more respectable and more in line with their new status as free Americans. Although slaves had surnames that were usually different from their master's, most slaveholders recognized a slave only by his or her first name. Sometimes slaves kept this surname, but often they changed both their first and second names. Sometime their surname reflected their complexion. There were thus many Browns and Blacks among the freed population. Sometimes the name reflected their occupation. For example, the literal meaning of Sojourner Truth is traveling preacher. Indeed, Truth's oratorical skills were renowned and she used them in the cause of Christianity as well as abolitionism and women's rights. Henry Mason, for example, was a bricklayer, Charles Green was a gardener, and Thomas Smith could have been a blacksmith or a silversmith. Other former slaves chose the names of liberty. There were names like Justice, and many chose the name Freeman as a mark of their new identity.

In addition to signifying a new identity, the name chosen by these free men and women reflected their evaluation of their chances of success. Those who took the name of their craft, for instance, probably felt good about prospering economically. The few like William Ellison, who took their master's name, no doubt saw advantages in their choices, too. In a world where a black skin was inhibiting, white men could ease the way to economic independence. Ellison knew this. His cotton gin-making business was built as much on his own skills as on the Ellison name, a

Many freed blacks— including the subject of this painting by Thomas Waterman Wood, Moses, the Baltimore News Vendor—*turned to the Bible when choosing a name.*

name associated with one of the wealthiest planters in a region where such wealthy planters had a need for his skill and product.

More than keeping his master's name, Ellison also kept his attachment to his master by staying fairly close to him, something most freed slaves avoided. Ellison's choice no doubt had a lot to do with the fact that his master was probably also his father. Though he did move about 50 miles to another town, this was far less of a move than that made by many freed people. Of course, runaways had to flee because their lives depended on it. But legally emancipated slaves also left the area where they had been enslaved. Some just needed to test their mobility as a way of demonstrating their liberty. Others migrated to areas where they knew they had friends and family. Still others left for only a short while, returning *because* of the familiarity they had with the area and the people. Above all, they tried to get out from under their former master's supervision. The best way to do that was to move.

And yet, for black Americans freedom did not mean total liberty. Those who moved to rural areas found it difficult to make freedom work for them. In the South, rural free blacks who were not attached to plantations as carpenters, blacksmiths, coopers (barrelmakers), and the like, rented land, equipment, and supplies and tried to eke out a living by growing and selling their crops. Very few were successful. White landowners charged exorbitant rates for the rental of land and just one mediocre harvest could put a free black family far into debt. African Americans in this situation were forced to go to prison or, to meet their debts, sign over their future crops to the landowner. In either case they became peons, people tied to the land. They either had to work forever for the person whose land they rented or be imprisoned. If they went to jail they were subsequently hired out and forced to work for the person the authorities had sold their labor to, to persons willing to pay their debts. Either way many rural free blacks found themselves in virtual servitude.

Faced with the choice of renting land under such unfavorable circumstances or signing labor contracts, most rural free blacks opted for the latter. But this too put them in slavelike circumstances. Most contracts specified that free Negroes work according to the same rules governing slave hands. Thus when Aaron Griggs hired himself to a Louisiana planter he pledged "to work as one of the hands of the plantation." He pledged also not to leave the plantation during his term of service, "to go out to the fields at the same hours with the people of the plantation & to work with the plantation overseer." In all likelihood Griggs got the same amount of food and clothing as the slaves, but since he had to pay for them at prices set by his employer he found himself at the end of the year in debt to the very person who he had worked for like a slave.

Free blacks who succeeded in the rural South were the rare exception. William Ellison falls into this category. His skill as a ginmaker made

him indispensable to white
planters. He was therefore
able to make freedom work
for him. But Ellison also
had other advantages.
He was light skinned,
and whites, especially
those in the Lower
South, showed a
definite tolerance
for blacks who were
close to them in skin
color.

A badge issued to a freed black living in Charleston, South Carolina. Both freed blacks and slaves were required to wear these identification badges.

It was not just a
matter of standards of
beauty. A light color signified a birth connection to a
white person. Although there were
enough whites who believed that one drop of Negro blood made one
a Negro, there were also many white men who had fathered mulattoes,
and some white women who had given birth to them. These white
parents were often reluctant to leave their children totally exposed
to racist hostility. They thus protected them by providing for some
education or training in a trade. The industriousness of these free persons of color made some white South Carolinians feel safe in their presence. As a group of white men who signed an 1822 Charleston petition
put it, mulattoes were "a barrier between our own color and that of the
black."

For sure, Ellison made the most of this sentiment. Records show,
for instance, that he was probably the son either of his master or of
his master's father. It was this blood connection that saved him from
becoming an ordinary field hand on the cotton plantations owned by
his relatives. That he took the name of his masters, and identified with
them in every way, even to the extent of holding slaves, is quite under-
standable.

Since most free blacks lacked Ellison's advantages, they had to find
other ways of surviving. In both the North and the South the cities held

White fathers seldom acknowledged their black children. This 1836 cartoon shows Richard Johnson, who was elected Vice President of the United States, with his two biracial daughters.

more opportunities for African Americans than rural areas did. This is where most of the unskilled jobs were, and since, unlike Keckley or Ellison, most free African Americans were unskilled laborers, the city was the place to find work.

It was also a place to find other free blacks and begin the task of making new friends and building a new life. In the cities free blacks had more choices than they had in rural areas. There they could join a black church and worship the way they wanted. They could send their children to a school set up by that church or the school established by the benevolent society that they might also belong to. In the city they could hold celebrations. They could go to the grog shops or bars, or attend a show, or even bury their dead in a service under their own direction. They could do so, moreover, away from the constant supervising eyes of white slaveholders.

Small wonder then that by 1860, on the eve of the Civil War, free blacks could be described as the most urban of all of America's people.

A railway conductor expelling a black man from a coach in Philadelphia.

In the South more than a third of the free-black population dwelled in cities or towns, although only 15 percent of the whites and about 5 percent of the slaves lived in cities. In the North, Boston, New York, Cincinnati, and Philadelphia held the bulk of the free-black population.

Opportunities prevailed in antebellum urban America but not without struggle. As in rural areas, blacks faced obstacles. Everywhere they turned they encountered white suspicion, competition, and hostility. Opposition to them was so fierce, and their freedom was so restricted, that like free rural African Americans it is more apt to describe their condition not as free but as quasi-free.

Most cities and states, in fact, tried hard to limit the size of the free-black population, and where possible, to eliminate it. This effort began early in the 1800s and could be traced to the waning of the revolutionary fervor over liberty, the rise of cotton, and the resulting demand for slaves. Specifically, as the nation settled into its growing-up stage, and as its economy became more and more fueled by the money made from cotton production, anything that threatened slavery, the institution upon which cotton production was based, was perceived as dangerous.

By white standards, therefore, free blacks were dangerous. They threatened to disrupt the existing order because they contradicted the pro-slavery argument that Negroes could not survive without white supervision. They also threatened slavery because they had a vested interest in slavery's elimination. Not only did most have bitter memories of their time in slavery, but most had relatives or friends still in bondage. Moreover, as long as slavery existed, and as long as most blacks were slaves, all blacks were presumed slave, even free blacks. Free African Americans therefore had every reason to want—and work toward—slavery's elimination.

Antebellum whites had a totally different mind-set. In the North, South, and West, whites who were skilled artisans and common workers feared free African Americans. Thanks to the 1820 Missouri Compromise, slavery was outlawed north of the 36th parallel. Northern and western white laborers, therefore, did not have to compete against slave labor, a competition they could never win because they could not sell their labor as cheaply as the slave who, of course, worked for nothing. The free black, though, was a formidable competitor because discrimination forced African Americans to sell their labor for less than it was worth. It was in the white laborer's interest, therefore, to eliminate all black competition however he could.

One way he did this was by refusing to work alongside blacks. Frederick Douglass ran into this problem when, as a fugitive from slavery, he moved to New Bedford, Massachusetts, and sought work as a caulker. Employers would not hire him because they risked losing all their white employees. As Douglass explained, "I was told by an anti-slavery ship builder there, who had a vessel on the stocks to be caulked, that if he should even venture to send me on that ship, every white man would leave him, and he could not get her ready for sea. Go where I would, I could not get employment at my trade." Ex-slave carpenter Henry Boyd had a similar experience in Cincinnati. After days of unsuccessful job hunting, he finally found an Englishman who would hire him. When he entered the shop, though, "the workmen threw down their tools, and declared that he should leave or they would. 'They would never work with a nigger.'"

Laws restricting the movement and rights of free blacks were as effective as such impromptu attempts to limit the freedom of African Americans. In the South free blacks were forced to carry certificates of freedom on their person. If caught without one there was the danger of being claimed as a slave. In many places free blacks had to register with the police or court authorities. South Carolina, for instance, required free people of color between the ages of 16 and 60 to pay a $2 tax each year. The tax enabled whites to know who was free and where free blacks lived. Like other Southern states, South Carolina also prohibited the migration of free blacks into the state, as well as the emancipation of slaves. These laws aimed to reduce the number of free blacks, and they did so very effectively.

A host of other laws were passed to curtail the rights of Southern free blacks. When free African Americans met in any numbers, even in church, they were required to have a white person in attendance. Southern laws also set curfews for black gatherings. Blacks were widely excluded from public parks and burial grounds, relegated to the balconies of theaters and opera houses, and barred from hotels and restaurants. Of all the Southern states only Maryland, Tennessee, and North Carolina gave free blacks the vote, but by 1835 all had repealed this right. To add insult to injury, no Southern court allowed them to serve on juries or give testimony in court against whites. And, if convicted of any crime, the punishment meted out to them was always more severe than that given to whites convicted of the same crime. Free blacks faced public whippings and, most ominous of all, enslavement, a fate whites never suffered.

Conditions in the non-slaveholding states were slightly better but got worse as one traveled from the Northeast to the Northwest. Slavery had been outlawed in the states of Ohio, Indiana, Illinois, Wisconsin, and Michigan by the Northwest Ordinance of 1787, but whites there were

A page from Baltimore's 1819 city directory. The dagger symbol was used to distinguish blacks from whites.

```
                 JON—JON

Jones, Rachel, widow, 39 German
      Mahler, cabinet maker, Gillingham's al.
      Elisha, fisherman, Cross f h
     †Matilda, laundress, Honey al. near Han-
        over st. f h
     †Isaac, grain measurer, s. end of s. How-
        ard
     †Jacob, stage driver, Harford extended o t
     †James, potter, Harford extended o t
     †Andrew, shoe black, cor. of Goodman st.
        and Sugar al.
     †Sarah, laundress, N. Calvert near Centre
      William, pilot, 57 Alisanna f p
      Barnard, ship carpenter, Fleet between
        Washington st. and Castle al. f p
      Owen, rigger, Wilk opposite the Methodist
        Church
      John, rigger, Argyle al. near Shakespeare
        f p
     †Thomas, laborer, Strawberry al. near Ger-
        man st. f p
     †George, laborer, Strawberry alley N. of
        Gough st f p
     †Joseph, cheese man, 17 George f p
     †Noah, carter, Union lane s. of Lexing-
        ton st.
     †James, barber, N. Eutaw s. of Franklin
     †Isaac, laborer, Larew's al.
     †Rebecca, laundress, 2 German lane
      Margaret, widow, boarding house, 66 Cum-
        berland row
      William, constable, 67 Harrison
      Ann, widow, 7 Conewago
      Lewis, boot and shoe maker, Cowpen al.
        near Liberty st.
      Henry, sawyer, French al.
      Margaret, binder, 20 Primrose al.
```

still prejudiced against blacks. As in the South, skilled laborers were especially fearful of black competition. To discourage black migration, Northwestern and Western states alike passed black codes that resembled the restrictive laws of slavery. Like Southern states they also required blacks to register their certificates of freedom at a county clerk's office, but here free blacks had to pay a bond of $500 or $1,000 guaranteeing that they would not disturb the peace or become a public charge. Illinois, Indiana, and Oregon actually excluded black migrants altogether.

1839.]   *Anti-Slavery Almanac.*   15

SCHOOL FOR COLORED GIRLS

Conditions for free blacks were probably the best in the Northeast, but even in these states restrictions were intolerable. Most qualified black voters lost the vote and social custom kept them off juries. What the law did not do, mob violence did. Blacks in Philadelphia suffered the fury of the mob as early as 1805, when dozens of white citizens turned on those gathered for a Fourth of July ceremony and drove them away from the festivities with a torrent of curses. During the 1830s and 1840s, riots occurred again in Philadelphia, and also in New York, Pittsburgh, Cincinnati, and Providence. In each case white mobs burned and looted black churches, meeting halls, and homes, and beat, stoned, and even murdered black citizens.

To survive, most African Americans found a way to work around white prejudice. Nowhere in the United States was this easy. In the Northeast, employment opportunities in the emerging industries went almost entirely to whites who used every means, including violence, to keep their economic advantage. Blacks could find jobs only at the bottom of the job ladder as common laborers. They loaded ships, dug wells, graves, and house foundations, and toiled as sweepers, porters, ashmen, chimney sweeps, and bootblacks.

Despite their free status, blacks in the Northern states were still subject to violent, racist attacks. This illustration shows a mob burning down a school for black children.

Paradoxically, economic opportunities increased for free blacks the further south one went into slave country. Not only were there fewer skilled and unskilled white immigrant laborers in the South, but white employers were accustomed to hiring blacks to do work that white men would not do. Free blacks, therefore, were able to eke out a living even though they faced competition from both slaves and native-born whites. For example, nowhere in the South would white men cut hair. Free blacks therefore acquired a monopoly on the barbering trade. In Charleston, skilled white carpenters, tailors, and millwrights were scarce, leaving these occupations to be filled by free blacks. Blacks also found employment in Southern industries, usually in the least-skilled positions. In Richmond, for instance, half the employed Negro men labored in tobacco factories, paper mills, and iron foundries.

Free-black urban women did not have as many opportunities as their male counterparts. Elizabeth Keckley was exceptional. Both North and South, few blacks owned their own businesses or commanded their own time. Most worked in the service trades as laundresses, cooks, and maids. Even in this kind of work they faced competition from native-born white women of the poorer classes, and as the period progressed, from immigrant women, especially those from Ireland. Like free-black men, though, they worked longer hours than the average white person, and longer hours than the average white woman, who often did not work at all. With some luck they managed to survive on their own.

In some cities they did quite well. In Richmond, Virginia, for instance, free-black women amassed property that exceeded the value of that amassed by their men. Most of the women there were domestic servants of some sort, but that did not stop them from buying their relatives out of slavery or from doing fairly well with limited opportunities.

Whether male or female, surviving in the city and surviving well meant being blessed with some amount of luck. Luck had different meanings for whites and free blacks. For the latter luck meant having a trade that was not taken over by white laborers. Luck also meant being able to support one's children so that officials could not force them into legal apprenticeships. Thousands of black parents in both the North and South had their children taken away and forced into 18 or 20 years of service because state or city officials deemed them unable or unfit to care for them. In Philadelphia, apprenticeship periods for blacks were sometimes as long as 28 years. Once in an apprenticeship black children seldom received the education or the training in a trade that white children received.

In light of all the restrictions on free blacks and the discrimination and prejudice they faced, it is worth remembering that they were not slaves. Although they were only semi-free, they were not in bondage. This status had real significance, significance a slave could appreciate. For, after all, free blacks could legally rename themselves. They could marry legally, and free women gave birth to free children. They had more opportunities to learn to read and write. For instance, although only one of Sojourner Truth's five children obtained any education, at least two of her grandchildren obtained literacy during the days of slavery. William Ellison's children were more fortunate than Truth's. He sent them to Philadelphia to be educated at the Lombard Street Primary School, a school run by Margaretta Forten, a free-black teacher.

Free blacks could also make their lives meaningful in ways slaves could not. Throughout the country free African Americans had more control over their religious practices. Shortly after Sojourner Truth was freed, she joined a Methodist congregation in Ulster, New York. Like thousands of free blacks, Truth found the more participatory, unconstrained emotional services of the Methodists more to her liking than the quiet, solemn services of other denominations.

For free blacks, though, it was not enough to be accepted in a white congregation. Even the Methodists often led segregated services and refused to allow blacks equal say in the governance of churches. Blacks who attended Episcopal, Baptist, and Presbyterian churches also encountered resistance when they tried to exercise control over the way they worshipped. Beginning, therefore, in the 1790s and continuing through the 1850s blacks struggled and achieved a measure of independence in their religious practices by founding their own churches.

Probably the first formal services were offered in 1791 in Philadelphia by the Free African Society under the leadership of Absalom Jones. After that, blacks all over the country founded their own churches, in buildings they owned, under ministers of their own choosing. They conducted their own marriage ceremonies, their own baptisms, their own burial rituals. Whites protested such independent black organizing, and especially in the South blacks encountered strenuous white resistance to black churches.

This 1829 etching shows a free black woman shopping in Philadelphia for "flesh coloured stockings."

In the end, however, white prejudice worked *for* African Americans. In the South, where laws prohibited black assembly, whites nevertheless shunned integrated worship with free African Americans. Yet, adopting the same reasoning they employed regarding slaves, whites believed that Christianity would make free blacks more controllable and less dangerous. Therefore, even though black churches were often raided and shut down by suspicious whites, between 1800 and 1860, and especially after 1840, independent African-American churches grew and thrived.

To the extent that the churches survived and prospered, so too did African-American communities. Just as it did for slaves, religion provided a psychic space and freedom found nowhere else. Like slaves, free blacks identified with the Jews of the Old Testament and believed that God would deliver them in this world and the next.

For free blacks, however, the church was a structure—an institution—in a way it was not for the slave. Besides being the one corner of the world where blacks went unhindered by whites, the church was the center of black life. Most black schools were founded by the black church. Most self-help activities were conducted through the church, and most positions of leadership in the community were held in the church. Not surprisingly, it was often the church's struggle for survival against white efforts to shut its doors that lent unity and solidarity to many African-American communities.

So much was dependent on the survival of the black church. Black schools offer a good example. In antebellum America in both the North

Under the leadership of Absalom Jones, the Free African Society began offering formal church services to blacks in Philadelphia in 1791.

The African Episcopal Church of St. Thomas, the first black church in the United States, was opened in Philadelphia in 1794.

and the South adult education was almost nonexistent, and black children were either given substandard education or were barred from public and private schools altogether. It was usually the church that took up this burden. In the North and the upper and border Southern states, African churches ran Sunday schools where children were encouraged to read the Bible. Most churches in these areas had day schools that children attended for free or for a small fee. In Baltimore, for example, Daniel Coker's school was attached to the Saratoga Street African Methodist Episcopal Church. By the end of the 1850s Baltimore had 15 African-American schools at the primary and secondary levels, with more than 2,600 students. Schools attached to the African Methodist Episcopal church were founded in Philadelphia and other cities.

In addition to the church, benevolent societies were a unifying element in free African-American society. One of the first was founded in Boston by Prince Hall, who before the American Revolution was granted a

> "Go ye into all the world and preach the Gospel to every creature." Mark xvi, 15.
>
> "Exhort with all long-suffering and doctrine."

This is to Certify, That the bearer *Benjamin J. Sa....* 18

is licensed to *Preach* in the AFRICAN METHODIST EPISCOPAL CHURCH: Signed in behalf of the *Quarterly* Conference of said Church, so long as his life corresponds with the Gospel and he submit to the rules of the Discipline of said Church.—To be renewed once a year,

Given under my hand, this *13th* day of *December* in the year of our Lord one thousand eight hundred and *58*

John Tibbs Parlor Wylie St. Charge P. Mabury

A preacher's license issued in 1858 by the African Methodist Episcopal Church. The AME originated in Philadelphia in 1786 under the leadership of George Allen. It quickly spread throughout the North.

charter from England to establish a Masonic lodge, a fraternal organization. In 1797 Hall presided over the installation of the first officers in Philadelphia's African Lodge of Pennsylvania. By 1815 there were four lodges in Philadelphia that had pooled their resources to build a black Masonic Hall.

Like benevolent societies in other cities in both North and South, these organizations provided services to their members as well as to the larger black community. For example, they provided disabled members with "sick dues" to assure them an income when they could not work, and they also gave elderly members money to live on. They organized the burial of their members, providing plots, headstones, and ceremonies for the departed. Some of the associations ran schools for orphan children and provided for companionship for the sick and disabled. Some workingmen's associations tried to secure better wages and job security, and still others functioned like Baltimore's Society for Relief in Case of Seizure, an organization that guarded against the kidnapping of free blacks into slavery.

These benevolent societies not only provide an excellent example of African-American self-help but also give us insight into the social organization of most African-American communities. In 1790 the Brown Fellowship Society of Charleston, South Carolina, was formed by five free men of color. Membership was limited to 50 persons, who had to pay an initial membership fee of $50 plus monthly dues. The fellowship used this money to provide for the funeral and burial expenses of its

In 1815, the New York Society for Promoting the Manumission of Slaves opened the New York Free African School to provide schooling to black children.

John Burns   The *performance* N° 2.   8

The New York African Free School,

ERECTED IN THE YEAR 1815.

By the

New York Society for promoting the Manumission

of Slaves.

Officers of the Society.

Cadwallader D. Colden President.

Valentine Seaman 1st Vice Pres.t; George Newbold 2nd Vice Pres.t

John Murray Jun.r Treasurer,

Jeremiah Thompson Secret.y, Thomas Tucker Assist. Secret.y

Trustees of the School.

John Murray Jun.r Chairman; Thomas Collins Secre.y

Benj.n S. Collins,   Robert C. Cornell,   S. F. Jenkins,

Walter Sawyer,   Willet Seaman,   Jeremiah Thompson,

Thomas Tucker,   William Waring,   George F. White,

Samuel Wood.

Teacher.

Charles C. Andrews.

members and monthly stipends for the widows and orphans of members. The society also provided for the care of some of the poor among Charleston's free-black population. Another society, also of Charleston, the Friendly Moralist Society, founded in 1838, functioned similarly. Yet another Charleston organization, the Humane Brotherhood, was formed in 1843, and it too provided sick benefits, burial expenses, and a fixed yearly income for widows and orphans of deceased members.

What makes these associations interesting is their organization around wealth and complexion. Obviously any free black who could afford the membership dues of these societies belonged to the exceptional class of free African Americans—people who, like William Ellison, had distinguished themselves from the masses of illiterate and unskilled free blacks. They owned property, were educated, and could provide for the education of their children, even if it meant sending them out of the state or even out of the country.

In every city, whether New York or New Orleans, there were classes of African Americans who were distinguished this way. They were the elite who succeeded despite all the obstacles placed in their way. In city after city they formed musical and literary societies. They preached a gospel of moral purity, and their social events were reported in black newspapers such as *Freedom's Journal*, first published by John Russwurm and Samuel Cornish in 1827 in New York City. They held themselves up to blacks and whites alike as the moral guardians of the race, the standard of excellence that all blacks could achieve if white prejudice disappeared.

These societies in Charleston were also notable because they were organized around color. Specifically, the Brown Fellowship and Friendly Moralist societies were exclusively for mulattoes, while the Humane Brotherhood was limited to no more than 35 "respectable Free Dark Men." This division of benevolent societies along color lines could be found everywhere in the United States, but it was especially pronounced in the Lower South, from South Carolina to Louisiana. It was in these states, where slavery was most entrenched, that the free-black population was the smallest and most restricted. Manumissions, even during the revolution, were never numerous, and slaves who were emancipated were very likely blood relatives of their master. In these states, mulattoes, usually called free people of color, were presumed by authorities to be free, and dark-skinned blacks, even those who were free, were presumed to be slaves.

In practical terms this meant that mulattoes had a better chance of surviving and succeeding than dark-complexioned blacks did. Often it was because their white relative gave them some advantage over other African Americans. In William Ellison's case it was an education and training as a cotton gin-maker; for others it included a ticket out of the South. The fact that whites were not as threatened by mulattoes as they were by the darker-skinned worked in the former's favor as well. Upper-class African-American society therefore was generally lighter than the poor, working, and middle classes.

And yet, the existence of the dark-skinned, upper-class Humane Brotherhood is evidence that wealth and good fortune were not always synonymous with a light skin. At the same time that many dark-skinned blacks excelled, southern plantations held many mulattoes in slavery. Some were so white that their African heritage was not obvious. For African-American women, light skin could bring dubious advantages. White men often found them desirable and this sometimes had its end in freedom for the mulatto woman, but more often than not, the result could be a lifetime of sexual exploitation. Mulatto women probably saw more house service than did their darker sisters, but house service was not always a blessing. Excessive supervision by whites, and exposure to the whims of the white owners, could prove more disastrous than field work.

In assessing the value of a light skin, Elizabeth Keckley's experience is instructive. She was enslaved for 30 years. During those years she was sold twice, became a slave mistress and bore a son fathered by her master, and was moved from the place of her birth twice before she finally bought her freedom. Her light skin may have helped her cultivate her dressmaking clientele but by no means did she lead an easy life. Nor did her color make her exceptional.

A light skin, therefore, could help with success, but other factors such as literacy, a trade or profession, and white connections helped structure free-black antebellum society. And structured it was. Differences in wealth, literacy, complexion, and occupation made for different social connections and classes within black society. It was not unusual for wealthier African Americans to attend a different church from those

of the middle and lower classes. Usually the wealthier the free black, the less emotional his religious denomination. Methodists and Baptists attracted the African-American masses, and those with skills, literacy, and wealth usually joined or formed their own more reserved Episcopal or Presbyterian church.

Despite the differences, though, despite their varied occupations and chances for success, freedom for African Americans was always and everywhere limited. White freedom and black freedom were never the same, and although there were many things to divide blacks from each other, their partial freedom brought them all together. As the nation moved closer to the Civil War, the more similar all black life became. In the North and West blacks became scapegoats for a conflict many wanted no part of. In the South, the color line that separated white from colored

An enthusiastic preacher inspires the congregation during a service in the African Church of Cincinnati, Ohio. Such displays of emotion and exuberance were seldom found in the church services of wealthier African Americans.

was drawn tighter so that all free people of color suffered severe restrictions on their freedom, limits resembling those placed on slaves.

Increasingly, men like William Ellison were unable to ignore the protests of men like the ex-slave and abolitionist Frederick Douglass. Increasingly, they had to take sides. In the South, where by 1860 the color line was drawn fast and tight, all free African-Americans—the light skinned and the dark, the skilled and the unskilled, the literate and the illiterate, the Episcopalian and the Baptist—faced the same hostile whites. As they raised their voices in protest in the years immediately preceding the Civil War they struck a chord of unity—unity with each other, and unity with the slave.

THE NORTH STAR.

RIGHT IS OF NO SEX—TRUTH IS OF NO COLOR—GOD IS THE FATHER OF US ALL, AND ALL WE ARE BRETHREN.

ROCHESTER, N. Y., FRIDAY, DECEMBER 22, 1848.

of the commune, to mark the contempt in which they were held, the collector was accompanied with a dog, to which each Cagot was obliged to give a piece of bread." In the towns, particular quarters were assigned them, and in country villages, they lived in separate hamlets. Sometimes the people were forbidden to employ them as labors.—By the municipal regulations of one place, they could not enter its limits without a badge of red cloth, to indicate their degradation; and if they met one of the town's people, they were obliged to stand on one side of the road till he passed. They were forbidden to touch the vessels out of which people drank, or to take water out of the public well. (In this place, colored people are prohibited from entering the public grounds about the Capitol, unless on necessary businss.) "In the earlier part of the seventeenth century, the inhabitants of Oleran complained, as of an intolerable nuisance, that some Cagots of that place had presumed to keep pigeons, which, leaving their homes in search of food, mixed with the pigeons of their neighbors; and at another place, a Cagot was punished for having been found fishing with a line in the river. (A slave boy in Georgetown, D. C., who should be found flying a kite, would be liable to a fine of two dollars, and, in default of payment, to whipping by the Mayor, at his discretion.) They were forbidden to enter any tavern. (Our free people of color are forbidden to keep taverns of any kind.)

In the *churches*, however, the prejudice was most fearfully manifested.—The following extract from the Edinburgh Review will remind one of the negro pew sand cemeteries of this country, only there is nothing in the bitterness, the antipathy against colored people, as shown in our churches, to equal the fiendish cruelty of the pious people of France and Spain, inflicted on this unfortunate *white* race.

"In some places they seem to have had at a remote period churches or chapels of their own—at least the ruins or traces of small ecclesiastical buildings are found, which popular tradition ascribes to them. In most of the churches of the west and southwest of France, there is a small entrance door, (now often walled up) called the Cagot's door, quite distinct from the principal entrance: there is also a division of the church at some distance from the portion of the church occupied by the congregation, which is understood to

strained, the cure' burst into a rage in the middle of the service, and shouted out, "Votre place n'est pas la, Cagot! et sachez que moi, que je soie devant ou derriere vous, je suis toujours votre cure; mais vous autres, que vous soyez devant ou derriere, vous ne serez jamais que de villains Cagots!"

"The prejudice against the Cagots was not confined to the interior of the church; for in almost every parish there was a separate cemetery for them or at least a place set apart for them in the cemetery belonging to the church; a person who was not a Cagot would not on any account be interred near thom."

People then were as ready in finding arguments to justify their antipathies, as they are now. At one time they would charge the Cagots with witchcraft; at another, they would denounce them as *lepers*, though not the slightest proof has ever been found to justify such denunciation. According to a popular tradition, still preserved in two or three places, they were the descendants of the carpenter who made the cross on which Christ was crucified—and the only reason that could be given for this was, that their occupation, as mechanics, was generally that of carpenter. In reply to a remonstrance uttered by them against the refusal of the clergy of Navarre to allow them t participate in the rites of the church the huisser of the Conseil Royal, in opposing their demands, traced their genealogy back to Gehazi, the wicked servant of Elisha, (as the Africans are said to be the descendants of Canaan, the cursed) "and as the prophet's curse was still hanging over them, he concluded them to be spiritually leprous and damned. One can see in all this, the propensity of human nature to seek justification for feelings, which no REASON can explain or authorize, in religious sanctions.

It is worthy of remark, that the proscribed races of white people, like the blacks among us, bore the contempt and persecution inflicted upon them, with wonderful patience; and, in a few instances where the attempt has been made to rescue the Cagot population from an intolerant neighborhood, by removing them to a distant part of the country, they always showed an eager desire to return to their native place.

In the beginning of the seventeenth century, the medical faculty undertook to undermine this unaccountable prejudice, by demonstrating that these Cagots were just like other people, and one may suppose that philanthropic

and difficulties shall furl off from their way like clouds before the coming sun. Sympathy and encouragement will come to them from unexpected sources. Old prejudices once loosened, will be swept away, like old piles of rubbish in a river bed, torn up by a spring freshet; each one swelling the force by which those below are to be overcome. Politicians and the press will not be long in finding motives of interest, if they have no higher, to take up their cause, and long before they now dare hope for it, their rights will be returned to them by the very hands which tore them away.

We hope our friends will every where renew with spirit the agitation for the amendment of the Constitution, to give the right of suffrage to the people of color. By proper exertions a mamoth petition can be rolled in upon the Legislature at the coming session, which shall astonish and intimidate its opposers in both parties. Let them see that we are in earnest, that we are willing to spend time and money and labor, to secure our object, and our request will be respectfully heard and considered. A hundred thousand names to such a petition would give weight to our arguments in their eyes. We believe that this number can be obtained, if every man and woman will do their duty. But if we fail to secure such an array, a half, a quarter, or even a tenth part of the number will make a powerful impression on the lawmakers of the State.

We are sometimes asked how we can demand a right for our colored brethren, which we would not advise them to exercise? Because it is their *right*. They should have the same opportunity with ourselves, of being their own judges whether to vote or not. They are men, equal in rights to all other men, and this disfranchisement is a denial of their equal manhood. It suggests and encourages insults and injuries to them in all other relations to society, and tends to destroy their self respect, and degrade them in the eyes of others. It is an act of injustice on our part, injurious to our own hearts, and a precedent to innumerable other wrongs, and must tend to create and foster a jealousy among its victims, toward the whites. It is a denial by our government of our own religious faith and political creed, and the support of a foolish aristocracy in our midst. We demand its repeal as an act of duty by the whites, of justice to the colored man, and a testimony of principle to the world, as we would demand the repeal of a law prohibiting the joining of Ro-

again! Those who have purchased their freedom live in constant fear of abduction. I have been awakened at the dead hour of night by the suplication of a domestic, that I would save her sister, whom the men were carrying off. Knowing she was free, I went with a friend in search of the captive; we found her in custody of two 'nigger hunters' who showed an advertisement, $50 bounty; they claimed her as a runaway; she protested by her tears and assertions that she was not a slave. Force was threatened; it would have been resisted at all hazards. A night of horror to this girl passed away. The light of day beamed upon the facts; she was free and proved it. How narrow her escape!—If carried far away her lips sealed in silence, when would her rescue arrive?—at the grave.

Shall I tell with what horror representatives at our court from foreign lands behold, at the seat of government the exibition of principles of this free republic, where all men are by nature born equal!

Even the citizens of the District have not nerve to behold the execution of their wishes. Mothers separated from their children, and the injunction not to put asunder what God has joined together, despised and rejected. Slaves are sent on pretence of business and when beyond the sound of shrieks and supplications, they are seized and borne away to the pen.

Here it is that fathers sell their own children and themselves rivet the manacles of slavery forever!

Had wealth been mine I could have consecrated it to a holy purpose. I could have saved some, who had learned to read the Bible and yield to its requirements, giving evidence by a christian walk of the sincerity of brofession; such I could have saved, not from servile labor, but from the posession of one whose motive was lust, whose cruelty worse than death! If nature or accomplishments adorn the female slave, it is only to make her the object of greater desire. I have urged the claims of humanity, of pity, and mercy, all in vain."

I well remember the incident to which Col. Ellsworth refers in the foregoing extract, for I was the friend who accompanied him to the house where these 'nigger hunters' had rudely entered, and claimed the sister recently returned from 'the free West' on a visit to her relatives in this city; nor shall I soon forget the feelings aroused by the impudent menacing demeanor of these men. They interogated as men hav-

AWAY WITH WAR!

Did you ever think of the evils of War? Did you ever realize that it was one of the greatest curses of mankind. Did you ever see that the practice of war filled the world with Blood, with Slavery, with Barbarism and every species of Misery; Yet this is the case; and, reader, are you not a military man, or guilty in some way of promoting War? If so, complain not of want, suffering, ignorance, or degradation. Oppressed Laboring man or Factory girl, don't murmur at your hard lot; if your politics, religion or social influence upholds war, the reproach falls upon your own head. You foolishly empty your own pockets and cause your own sufferings. Benevolent man, Philanthropist — do you favor armies, navies, and military governments? Wonder not, then, at the depravity of man and the slow progress of truth and righteousness. Your self-contradiction and inconsistency in sustaining the custom of war, swells the current of wickedness more than pour good efforts can that of righteousness.

What has War done?—Evil, evil! It has done nothing but evil! It has destroyed human life, property, virtue and happiness Nothing else has it aimed to do. Drunkenness, profanity and licentiousness have been its legitimate products. Widows, orphans, paupers, beggars it has multiplied. Dr. Dick essimates that *fourteen thousand millions* of human beings have been slaughtered by war—inhabitants enough to people 18 worlds like the Earth! Think of this. What greater curse could wickedness invent? Plague, Pestilence and Famine have followed in its track; but these of themselves have not begun to equal war in their number of victims. Had Hyenas, Tigers, Panthers and Serpents been the world's only inhabitants, they would not have equaled Man in the destruction of life. What a field of human bones! What a sea of human blood!

What has War cost?—The mere money cost of war has been enough to pauperize the world. According to reliable estimates the present unpaid War Debt of Europe and the United States, incurred within the last 160 years, is about *Seven Thousand Million Dollars!* The annual interest of this debt, including the expenses of the Army and Navy, is nearly *Four Hundred Million Dollars*. The specie circulation of the world does not equal this amount, and, according to Hum-

CHAPTER 6
LET MY PEOPLE GO
◇ ◇ ◇

In 1847 the first edition of Frederick Douglass's newspaper, the *North Star,* rolled off the presses. It was not the first African-American newspaper nor would it be the last. And like the names of many other African-American publications, *North Star* signified black aspirations, because the North Star, the light that guided so many runaways out of the South, symbolized freedom.

In his dedication Douglass tied the fate of all blacks together, the free and enslaved, those north and those south. "We are one," he declared, "our cause is one" and "we must help each other." Douglass went on to declare the unity of the free black with the slave. "What you suffer, we suffer; what you endure, we endure. We are indissolubly united, and must fall or flourish together."

Douglass's words were prophetic, but it did not take a prophet to see the wisdom of his remarks. The nation was just 13 years from the Civil War. Already the ferment was rising. The American Antislavery Society was 14 years old. Founded by blacks and whites, the society held religious revival-style meetings where abolitionists made stirring speeches condemning slavery as a moral wrong. They urged their listeners to put pressure on state legislatures to end slavery. The abolitionist movement spawned the Liberty party, and in 1840 and 1844 it ran antislavery Presidential candidates. Although the Liberty party did not attract a significant following, it did plant the seed of fear of "slave power." The admittance of Texas into the Union as a slave state in 1845 and the promised addition of slave states from the territories taken by

The front page of The North Star, *a newspaper published by Frederick Douglass. The masthead stated, "Right is of no sex, truth is of no color, God is the Father of us all, and all we are brethren."*

A large crowd of both blacks and whites gathers in Boston for an anti-slavery meeting in 1841.

the United States as a result of the Mexican War in 1846 did in fact convince many Northerners that slaveholders would use their political and economic power to make slavery legal everywhere. More and more, Northern whites wondered whether slavery would or could be confined only to the South; more and more they wondered about the fate of white laborers in a slave labor economy.

Blacks, too, pondered their fate. But for them, the issues were different. Most important, the concerns of African Americans did not divide them as much as the debate over slavery divided whites. They had much to gain from white conflict over slavery, and they understood that they would not benefit at all if they were not united. And for the most part they spoke with one voice. Free blacks, those who could speak out against injustice, all wanted freedom for the enslaved and justice for the free. All wanted blacks to have the rights that were accorded by the Constitution to all Americans. They differed, however, on the means to achieve these ends. The story of black protest in the years before the

Civil War is one of unity on the large issues of rights and debate about the way to achieve them.

Black protest against slavery began long before the 1833 formation of the predominantly white American Antislavery Society. During the revolution the Continental Congress was bombarded with petitions from Northern slaves who used the "all men are created equal" clause of the Declaration of Independence to claim their freedom. Protest against slavery continued through the Confederation period, and at the beginning of the 19th century the African Methodist Episcopal minister Absalom Jones walked the streets of Philadelphia carrying a petition that protested the renewal of the slave trade in Maryland, the birthplace of many Philadelphia blacks. In their churches and benevolent societies African Americans raised money to help runaways, wrote petitions protesting slavery, and spoke against black bondage whenever and wherever the opportunity arose.

On a more subtle level, blacks celebrated New Year's Day as their Independence Day. As Frederick Douglass noted, to the slave the national Fourth of July celebration was a day that revealed "the gross injustice and cruelty to which he is the constant victim." To the slave, the shouts of liberty and equality, the prayers, hymns, sermons, and thanksgivings were "hollow mockery . . . mere bombast, fraud, deception, impiety, and hypocrisy—a thin veil to cover up crimes which would disgrace a nation of savages." New Year's Day, in contrast, had real meaning for African Americans. It was the anniversary of Haitian independence in 1804 and the end of the foreign slave trade with the United States in 1808.

As each New Year's Day passed, free blacks increasingly condemned the federal government for its perpetuation of slavery. They did not have to go much further than the Constitution to find a federal document worthy of condemnation. The Constitution allowed the foreign slave trade to persist for 20 years after its signing. For purposes of representation, it counted enslaved African Americans as three-fifths of a person. It also promised to put down slave insurrections and to track down fugitives from slavery and return them to their owners. This last provision, which put the federal government in the business of slave catching, was reinforced by a fugitive slave law in 1793 and by a particularly harsh one in 1850. African Americans vigorously opposed these laws, but between 1836 and 1844 the House of Representatives adopted

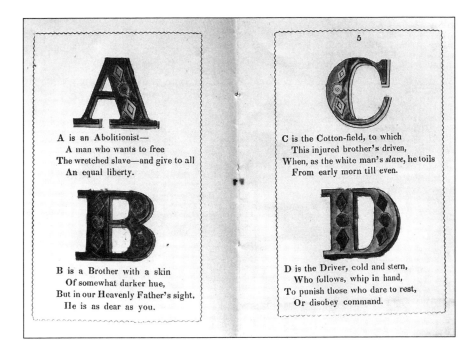

A is an Abolitionist—
A man who wants to free
The wretched slave—and give to all
An equal liberty.

B is a Brother with a skin
Of somewhat darker hue,
But in our Heavenly Father's sight,
He is as dear as you.

C is the Cotton-field, to which
This injured brother's driven,
When, as the white man's *slave*, he toils
From early morn till even.

D is the Driver, cold and stern,
Who follows, whip in hand,
To punish those who dare to rest,
Or disobey command.

The Anti-Slavery Alphabet, published in 1847, used simple rhymes to expose children to the horrors of slavery.

a "gag rule" against all antislavery petitions. Under this rule all abolitionist petitions were automatically tabled so that they could not even be discussed on the floor of the House.

Still blacks protested. They took particular aim at the program of the American Colonization Society. Founded in 1816, this society counted some of America's most notable citizens among its members. Presidents James Madison and Andrew Jackson, Senator Daniel Webster, and Francis Scott Key, author of "The Star-Spangled Banner," all argued that blacks should be returned to Africa because it was the only natural home of black people. Central to their argument was their belief that blacks would never be accepted in America. According to national leader and Presidential hopeful Henry Clay, the "Great Compromiser," blacks would ever inhabit "the lowest strata of social gradation." In his opinion blacks were "aliens—political-moral-social aliens, strangers, though native." Africa, on the other hand, held hope for blacks. It was a place where they would not be degraded and debased. Moreover, advocates of colonization believed that American Negroes, having come under the civilizing influence of Christianity and having observed the benefits of democracy and capitalism, would redeem Africa. They argued that African Americans would transform Africa into prosperous mini-American black republics. Colonization would open up new commercial routes between Africa and America. In short, what blacks could not do here in America, they could and would do in Africa. In their minds, the end result of colonization would benefit both blacks and whites, America and Africa.

And they used all kinds of pressure tactics to make African Americans see things their way. Convinced that blacks had to be indoctrinated at an early age, John H. B. Latrobe, a leading Baltimore colonizationist, wrote a children's primer that extolled the virtues of Africa and identified it as the only homeland of black people. The book even had a short hymn that children were encouraged to sing:

In 1808, at New York City's African Church, the Reverend Peter Williams, Jr., delivered this oration calling for an end to the slave trade.

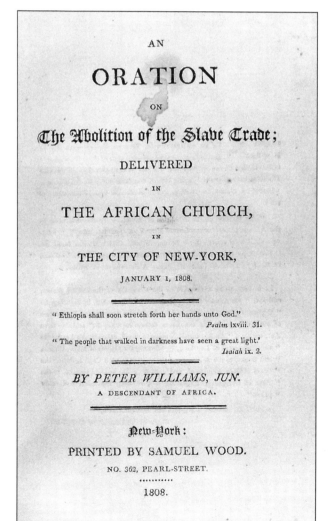

AN

ORATION

ON

The Abolition of the Slave Trade;

DELIVERED

IN

THE AFRICAN CHURCH,

IN

THE CITY OF NEW-YORK,

JANUARY 1, 1808.

" Ethiopia shall soon stretch forth her hands unto God."
Psalm lxviii. 31.

" The people that walked in darkness have seen a great light.'
Isaiah ix. 2.

BY PETER WILLIAMS, JUN.
A DESCENDANT OF AFRICA.

New-York:

PRINTED BY SAMUEL WOOD.

NO. 362, PEARL-STREET.

1808.

Land of our father, Af-ri-ca
We turn our thoughts to thee—
To gain thy shores we'll gladly bear
The storm upon the sea.

Colonizationists also tried to recruit well-known, successful blacks to lead the exodus to Africa. The most common strategy was to lure influential black leaders with the prospect of power, wealth, and prestige. For example, they offered James Forten, a wealthy sailmaker, commercial advantages if he would lead blacks back to West Africa. He refused, but it did not stop colonizationists from sensationalizing the advantages of going to Africa.

All but a few declined the opportunity to return. Those who did leave settled on land near the British colony of Sierra Leone. Located on land purchased by the American Colonization Society in 1822, the colony was named Liberia, the "land of freedom." It was the hope of settlers that this small country would fulfill the promise of its name and provide the liberty that America withheld. Certainly this was the hope of two of its most renowned settlers,

John Latrobe was one of the leaders of the American Colonization Society, which encouraged blacks to return to Africa.

Paul Cuffee, a black sea captain and ship owner, and John Russwurm, an educator and the editor of *Freedom's Journal*. Both men endorsed colonization because they felt America would never treat its black citizens fairly. "If the slaves of our country with one accord were delivered from bondage," Russwurm asked, "can they be elevated to an equality with the whites? Can they while in this country be divested of the odium of inferior and degraded caste?" The answer Russwurm had to his own question was "No!" For him and his small following, Liberia would provide the liberty denied by America.

The flag of Liberia was patterned after the flag of the United States.

But only a few people were willing to follow him. News of the troubled relationships that the settlers had with surrounding African tribes and the difficulty American blacks had with African diseases thwarted settlement. However, the most important reason why African Americans refused to return to Africa was their feeling that America was their country. Africa was indeed their *ancestral* homeland, but America was their birthplace and from it they drew their identity. They had fought and died in America's wars, had cleared this country's land and swamps, had helped build up its towns. The world, not just America, grew rich off the cotton, rice, and sugar grown by black people. They believed they had proved themselves productive, self-sufficient citizens, more so than even the slaveholder who had fewer skills, and who lived off the labor of others. To be asked to leave after such sacrifice to America was sheer injustice.

Many African Americans also believed that this push by whites exposed unadulterated white racism. White immigrants, they argued, were treated far better than they were. Immigrants met with less discrimination in the labor market, and once they qualified for citizenship were accorded all rights, including the vote. African Americans, on the other hand, were shut out.

African Americans asked that they be allowed to live free in this land that was the beacon of liberty. They protested the colonizationists' claim that blacks were incapable of living in freedom. They challenged

Guadillar Farm, a village in Liberia founded by black American settlers. More than 11,000 settlers were transported to Liberia by the American Colonization Society.

America to stand by its principles of democracy and liberty. When, in the early 1840s, the sixth federal census reported that blacks had a higher instance of insanity and idiocy than whites, James McCune Smith, a respected black physician, responded in a letter to the *New York Tribune*. "Freedom," he countered, "has not made us mad, it has strengthened our minds by throwing us upon our own resources and has bound us to American institutions with a tenacity which nothing but death can overthrow."

He might also have argued that African-Americans' minds had been strengthened to the point where they could discern a malicious plot when they saw one. They felt that colonization was just another means of depriving blacks of their rights as Americans. If blacks could succeed in Africa, in fact turn the entire continent into a replica of America, why could they not succeed here in America? The answer was sound and simple. Colonization was a way of getting rid of *them,* free blacks. More than any group in America they had a vested interest in opposing slavery. Slaves could not mount a sustained collective attack against slavery, but free blacks could and did. They wrote pamphlets, edited newspapers, collected money, hid runaways. Denmark Vesey organized a revolt.

Free blacks understood that it was their organized opposition to slavery that was threatening. Prominent among the leaders and members of colonization societies were slaveholders, none of whom supported the emancipation of slaves and their return to Africa, but all of whom argued that blacks were unprepared for freedom. In the opinion of most African-American leaders, colonization was a scheme to protect slavery and preserve freedom for whites only. Their fight against colonization, therefore, was a fight for themselves but also for their brothers and sisters in slavery. To leave America would be to accept the colonizationist view that free blacks were incapable of self-direction. It would also be an act of betrayal to the millions of their people who were enslaved. As they saw things, they were the slave's best hope, and the slave was their best ally in the cause of black rights.

Not that they did not want to forge alliances with white Americans, too. These were more problematic, however. For one thing, most prominent African-American leaders were dismayed by the widespread support given to colonization societies. Before the 1830s men like William Lloyd

John Russwurm and Samuel Cornish were the founders of America's first black newspaper, Freedom's Journal, *which began publication in March 1827.*

Garrison, Gerrit Smith, Arthur and Lewis Tappan, and Benjamin Lundy—whites who actively opposed slavery—also supported colonization. They did not see how colonization helped preserve slavery, or how the scheme exposed free blacks to the rage of anti-black mobs.

Such a mob let loose its venom in Cincinnati in 1829. Tension in the city had been growing throughout the 1820s. As the free-black population increased and competed for jobs, whites demanded their expulsion. They were encouraged by the leaders of the Cincinnati Colonization Society. Since its founding in 1826, it had prompted ministers and local newspapers to agitate against the city's blacks. Its propaganda provided the justification for driving them from the city. In the summer of 1829 city officials tried to push African Americans out by enforcing the Ohio Black Laws, which required blacks to post bonds guaranteeing "good behavior." Before black leaders could get a reprieve from the city legislature, white mobs attacked defenseless blacks. More than half the black population fled to Canada and other parts of the United States.

Although this and similar incidents convinced some sympathetic whites that colonization was inherently evil, it did not alter their prejudice towards blacks. This was another reason that African-American leaders found alliances with whites problematic. For example, even though black abolitionists like Peter Williams and William Watkins coaxed white men like William Lloyd Garrison and Gerrit Smith away from colonization, when Garrison and a small group of white friends met to organize the New England Antislavery Society in 1832, they invited blacks to join them only after all their plans had been formulated. Similarly, only 3 blacks were among the 62 signers of the American Antislavery Society's Declaration of Sentiments. Though it had 26 vice presidents and a 9-member executive committee, the society had no black officers.

African-American leaders were further disturbed by the limited perspectives and goals of white abolitionists. As free blacks they spoke against slavery as well as blanket discrimination against all blacks. White abolitionists, they found, were not much concerned with racism. Many black abolitionists shared the reaction of Theodore Wright, who criticized the "constitutions of abolition societies, where nothing was said about the improvement of the man of color!" Speaking before the New York Antislavery Society in 1837, Wright complained that "they have

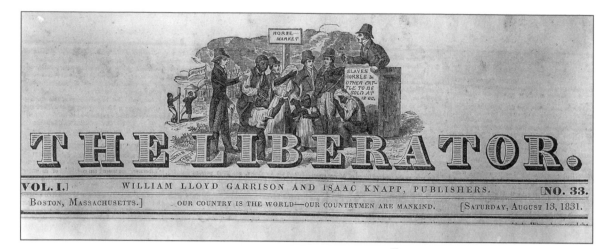

VOL. I.] WILLIAM LLOYD GARRISON AND ISAAC KNAPP, PUBLISHERS. [NO. 33.

BOSTON, MASSACHUSETTS.] OUR COUNTRY IS THE WORLD—OUR COUNTRYMEN ARE MANKIND. [SATURDAY, AUGUST 13, 1831.

The masthead of The Liberator, *an abolitionist newspaper published by William Lloyd Garrison and Isaac Knapp. Few white abolitionist groups included significant numbers of blacks in their groups.*

overlooked the giant sin of prejudice. They have passed by this foul monster, which is at once the parent and offspring of slavery."

Black abolitionists further noted that many white abolitionists refused to admit black children to their schools, would not hire black workers for anything but menial jobs, and even failed to hire blacks to work in antislavery offices. They also observed that in the early stages of their efforts, white abolitionists did not hire black lecturers, and when they eventually did they tried to control every aspect of their language and message.

A case in point involved Frederick Douglass. When Douglass first began lecturing in 1841 he related the trials of his slavery and the terrors of the institution. Garrison and others were pleased. They encouraged Douglass to repeat his performance over and over. As Douglass matured as a speaker, and as he pondered the meaning of freedom for himself and the nation, he grew more philosophical and learned in his talks. White abolitionists found Douglass the philosopher to be less "authentic" than Douglass the ex-slave. They did not want him to grow. Instead they repeatedly criticized him for appearing too smart. At one point he was told, "People won't believe you ever were a slave, Frederick, if you keep on this way. . . . Better have a *little* of the plantation manner of speech than not."

But Douglass, like other African-American leaders, listened to his own voice, and his own people, and in a very short time went his own way. Blacks continued to build their own movement. Central to it was

This rare 1850 photograph shows Frederick Douglass, seated to the left of the speaker's table, at an outdoor abolitionist meeting in Cazenovia, New York.

the black press. Newspapers founded by leading personalities reminded black Americans of their role in the development of the American nation. There was no lack of articles on the role black soldiers played in the American Revolution and the War of 1812.

At the same time that newspapers confirmed the black's identity as an American, they also grounded that identity in the black experience. Thus in their reporting of slave resistance, the terrors of slavery, and the free-black communities' assistance to fugitive slaves, newspapers made it difficult for free blacks to forget their relatively privileged status in relation to the slave. Just as important, these accounts helped cement the bond between slave and free.

Newspapers with such names as *The Colored American,* the *Weekly Advocate,* the *New Era,* and the *Weekly Anglo-African* helped unify African Americans by keeping them informed of the happenings in their own community and the nation. Articles and advertisements covering their various concerts, lectures, church events, educational opportunities, and school programs were regular features of black newspapers. By reporting national events from a black perspective and accepting editorials from ordinary African Americans, these newspapers allowed blacks to express their ideas on a variety of subjects and vent frustrations that had no other outlet. Since only a small percentage of the African-American population was literate, and these privileged few had to read or otherwise communicate the newspaper's contents to those who could not read, newspapers helped forge the bonds of community. They bridged the gap between the educated and the illiterate.

Through their own newspapers and a few edited by white abolitionists, ordinary African Americans learned of the protest activity of their leaders—men and women such as Douglass, Martin Delany, Henry Highland Garnet, William Wells Brown, William Whipper, and Maria Stewart. The question was how blacks should obtain their freedom. The decision was not an easy one. Would armed rebellion succeed? From their relatively safe surroundings, should they encourage the slaves to risk everything in a break for freedom? How far should free blacks go in opposing the fugitive slave laws? Should they hold off slave catchers with guns or would civil disobedience be enough? How would they achieve their rights of full citizenship?

Answers to these questions came from many quarters. In his speeches and in a pamphlet entitled *Walker's Appeal . . . to the Colored Citizens of the World But in Particular and Very Expressly to those of the United States of America,* David Walker urged African Americans to meet the slaveholders' violence with violence of their own. He blamed the oppression of blacks on white greed for money and power. In the by-now-typical African-American tradition of blending the secular with the sacred, of using religion to help solve life's problems, Walker urged black people to rise up and wage a holy war against whites, who had by their sin against African Americans sinned against God. "They want us for their slaves," he wrote. They "think nothing of murdering us in order to subject us to that wretched condition." In his justification of armed resistance, Walker wrote, "It is no more harm for you to kill a man who is trying to kill you, than it is for you to take a drink of water when thirsty: in fact the man who will stand still and let another man murder him is worse than an infidel."

No doubt many African Americans felt the same way Walker did, but most spoke with more moderate voices. Although they did not lose sight of the role played by whites in black oppression, many leaders urged African Americans to take an active role in liberation by uplifting themselves. Maria Stewart, one of the few African-American female public lecturers, urged blacks to give up drinking and invest in schools and seminaries. An admirer and follower of Walker, Stewart nevertheless believed that "nothing would raise our respectability, add to our peace and happiness, and reflect so much honor upon us, as to be ourselves the promoters of temperance, and the supporters . . . of useful and scientific knowledge." An advocate of female education during a time when it was thought that women best served the race by serving their husbands, brothers, and fathers, Stewart argued that the race needed both men and women in public roles. "Daughters of Africa" needed to unite. They could raise money to build schools to educate black youth, they could own stores that would service their community, they could educate themselves and through them the race would be uplifted.

As despairing as Stewart sometimes was when she looked at the plight of African Americans, she, like many others, was still more optimistic about the future than David Walker was. The goal of uplift was, after all, eventual integration into American life. Blacks were behind not because of natural inferiority but because of prejudice and slavery. Once these impediments were abolished, education and opportunity would remedy the situation.

Throughout the 1830s and 1840s Frederick Douglass shared Stewart's optimism. He did not support armed resistance or programs to go back to Africa. He believed that through constant preaching, political lobbying, and hard struggle blacks would eventually find liberty in America. "You must be a man here," he insisted, "and force your way to intelligence, wealth and respectability. If you can't do that here, you can't do it there." An 1840 editorial in the *Colored American* expressed a similar belief. Where else would people of color raise themselves politi-

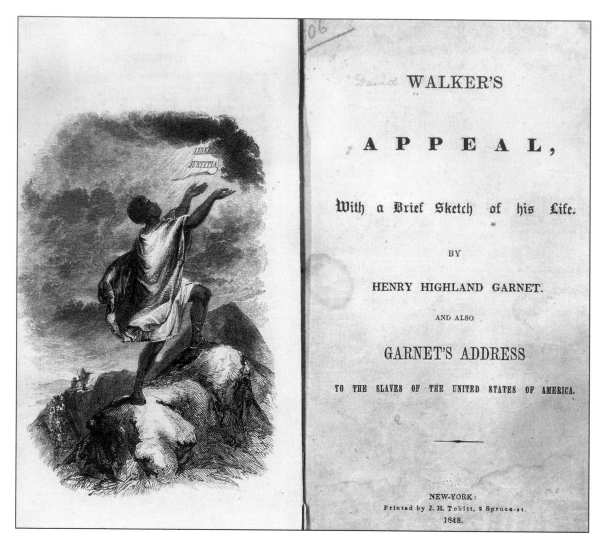

In Walker's Appeal, *a pamphlet published in 1829, David Walker, an outspoken orator and essayist, urged blacks to strike back violently against slaveholders and whites. This edition was published in 1848.*

cally, morally, and socially but in America? If America was at present an asylum of liberty and opportunity for whites only, at some point it would also embrace the African American.

But there were many who disagreed. Martin Delany, a Harvard-educated physician, was the most articulate spokesman against the views Douglass and others expressed. "No people can be free who themselves do not constitute an essential part of the *ruling element* of the country in which they live." These words, published in his 1852 book entitled *The Condition, Elevation, Emigration, and Destiny of the Colored People of the United States*, were part of his argument for emigrating from the eastern United States to Central or South America or to some nonsettled area in the American West. He did not share with Douglass the belief that America would allow blacks to become citizens. Much like Native Americans, blacks, he wrote, were "a nation within a nation." Blacks and whites shared a common country. But whites were an oppressor nation and blacks the oppressed nation. Black people, he claimed, loved America, but because that love was met with only belittlement and degradation, black people were "politically not of them, but aliens to the laws and privileges of the country." Thus separated, African Americans had a duty to establish a black society where they would be free to enjoy the privileges of citizenship.

Martin Delany, a Harvard-trained doctor, believed that African Americans should move out of the United States to Central or South America, places where he thought that they could establish a black society where they could enjoy the benefits of full citizenship.

These, then, were the lines of protest in African-American communities before 1850. Despite their different levels of optimism and different strategies of resistance, antebellum black leaders were united in their good feelings about themselves. Never did they give in to self-hatred, nor did they ever believe the pro-slavery arguments that held that they were naturally inferior to whites. Before America they stood tall and proud.

It was this black pride that eventually drove all black abolitionist leaders to advocate some degree of black separatism. In their minds, blacks, as a people, had to do for themselves; self-improvement had to be based on self-reliance. Said Phillip A. Bell, in the *Weekly Advocate*, whites may make "OUR CAUSE" their cause all they want, but their efforts will be unavailing "without our thinking and acting, as a body, for ourselves."

In thinking and acting for themselves blacks met during the 1830s through the 1850s in black-only national conventions. Northern cities such as Albany, Rochester, Cincinnati, Philadelphia, Buffalo, and Cleveland were the sites of some of the meetings where the means of uplift and strategies of resistance were debated. Although those who attended these conventions realized that some might think that all-black meetings worked against the goal of integration of blacks into the American mainstream, most concluded that racial solidarity was necessary to secure their status as full-fledged Americans. Separatism, whether in conventions, schools, or churches, was not the end in itself, but the means to the end.

For all of their work, it was, in the end, not black or even white abolitionists who struck the fatal blow against slavery. The institution proved so entrenched that it took a civil war to end it. Black protesters, however, could be proud of the work they did in unifying the spirits of free blacks and in forging the bond between free and enslaved African Americans. In so doing, they laid the intellectual foundation on which the protest of future generations of blacks and whites was built.

THE
AMERICAN ANTI-SLAVERY
ALMANAC,
FOR
1843.

BEING THE THIRD AFTER BISSEXTILE, OR LEAP YEAR ;
AND UNTIL JULY 4th, THE SIXTY-SEVENTH
OF THE INDEPENDENCE OF THE
UNITED STATES.

Oh, hail Columbia ! Happy land !
　The cradle land of Liberty !
Where none but negroes bear the brand,
　Or feel the lash of slavery.

Then let the glorious anthem peal !
　And drown, "Britannia rules the waves"—
Strike up the song that men can feel—
　"Columbia rules three million slaves !" Dr. Madden.

COMPILED BY L. M. CHILD.

NEW-YORK:
Published by the American Anti-Slavery Society, 143 Nassau street,
New-York ; 25 Cornhill, Boston ; and 31 North
Fifth street, Philadelphia.

Samuel B. Eastman, Printer.

CHAPTER 7

FROM DESPERATION
TO HOPE

◇ ◇ ◇

A t the end of 1850 African Americans did not know that the nation was just a decade away from civil war, that slavery would be its cause, or that the war would end slavery for good. They could not know that it would be the bloodiest war ever fought on America's soil or that their citizenship and voting rights would hang in the balance.

However, black people could not help but sense that something out of the ordinary was happening. Slavery was at the heart of heated discussions about the nation's future, and the Compromise of 1850, meant to quell anxiety about the slavery question, actually fanned its flames. The Compromise brought California into the nation as a free state, eliminated the slave trade in the District of Columbia, and organized the territories of Utah and Mexico. Its most obnoxious part was the Fugitive Slave Law. Under its harsh provisions, the law forced blacks accused of being fugitives to prove their free status, not to a jury, but to a special commissioner who was paid more ($10) for returning a slave to his owner than for setting him or her free ($5). The law also compelled Northerners to hunt down and turn in runaway slaves.

As slave hunters known as "kidnappers" flooded the North seizing fugitives, blacks had to decide what to do. They had always resisted fugitive slave laws, but by putting a bounty on every runaway's head, and making every white person a potential slave catcher, this latest fugitive law made resistance more risky and life for free blacks terribly

The American Anti-Slavery Almanac was published yearly by the American Anti-Slavery Society from 1836 to 1847.

An abolitionist pamphlet from 1839 contained this engraving of a free black man being kidnapped and sold into slavery.

insecure—so insecure that many free blacks took one last stride toward freedom by fleeing across the Canadian border.

The vast majority who remained faced a nation racked with conflict that did not lessen. Not a year passed that did not bring some event that forced slaves and free blacks to think hard about their future in America. No one—not William Ellison, Elizabeth Keckley, Sojourner Truth, Frederick Douglass, or Martin Delany—was spared the tough decisions the events forced. Abraham Lincoln's election to the Presidency in 1860 brought some hope that liberation was on the horizon. Mostly though, there was despair over the way the decade had proceeded and wretched bitterness over the country's betrayal of blacks.

Ironically, the 1850s was a decade of prosperity. Not only whites but blacks, too, did relatively well. This was indicated by the steady increase in black land and property ownership all over the country. In Nashville, for example, in 1860 there were 26 free blacks who were worth more than a thousand dollars who had owned no property 10 years earlier. Charleston had always had a wealthy colored elite, but during the 1850s as many as 75 whites rented their homes from freemen. In Baltimore free blacks monopolized the caulking trade, and throughout the Upper South free-black agricultural laborers took advantage of the movement of slaves south by demanding and receiving higher wages.

Economic success generated confidence. This confidence was visible in the new churches being built by larger and wealthier black congregations in the North and the South. It was also shown by the increased audacity of free blacks. In Petersburg, Virginia, for example, whites complained that blacks were slow to give way to whites on walkways. Expressing the opinion of the populace, a Petersburg editorial complained, "We see many of them with cigars, puffing their disgusting smoke into the faces of ladies and gentlemen . . . with a degree of *sang froid* [coldbloodedness], which even the Boston community would not tolerate in a white person."

Blacks also exuded more confidence in the way they responded to oppression. In Richmond, for instance, free blacks petitioned the city council to repeal the city's repressive Black Code, and in New York City there was the stunning behavior of Elizabeth Jennings. On a Sunday morning in 1854 she was pulled out of a horse-drawn trolley car and wrestled to the ground by a white conductor and driver who sought to keep her from sitting in the white section. With the same conviction and audacity shown by the free blacks of Richmond, Jennings took her case to court. Her victory there broke the back of segregation on public conveyances in New York.

John and Mary Jones of Chicago were among the nation's wealthiest free blacks and were nationally known abolitionists.

All over the country blacks tried to do the same to the Fugitive Slave Law. Twice in Boston, blacks and whites stormed a courthouse in failed attempts to rescue Thomas Sims in 1851 and Anthony Burns in 1854. Others, such as Elijah Anderson, John Mason, and of course, Harriet Tubman, continued to risk life and limb going into the South and delivering African Americans from slavery. Frederick Douglass also risked harm by his resistance to the law. Though very much in the public eye, he, like countless others, raised money for fugitives, hid them in his Rochester home, and helped hundreds escape to Canada.

And, like others, he had to struggle with the meaning of the Fugitive Slave Law. In Rochester, New York, in 1853 Douglass and other black abolitionists held one of their largest conventions to try to decide what to do about resisting the law. Reluctant though they were to call for the creation of separate black institutions, they felt the Fugitive Slave Law left them no choice. America seemed determined to cast them aside and destroy their rights as citizens. Somehow, they had to salvage them. In their attempt to do this, black abolitionists called for the creation of a national council to oversee black improvement and a manual labor school for the education of black children in science, literature, and the mechanical arts. They did this, they said, not to "build ourselves up as a distinct and separate class in this country but as a means to . . . equality in political rights, and in civil rights, and in civil and social privileges with the rest of the American people."

Although black abolitionists as a group took larger strides toward separatism, some individuals spoke out in favor of armed resistance. Douglass was among them. He not only increased his aid to fugitive slaves but he became decidedly more militant: "The only way to make the Fugitive Slave Law a dead letter is to make a half dozen or more dead kidnappers." For Douglass, black men had to prove that they were brave and not cowards; the future of the race depended on its men proving their mettle. His advice, therefore, was for "every colored man in the country" to "keep his revolver under his head, loaded and ready for use." In his mind, "every slave hunter who meets a bloody death in his infernal business, is an argument in favor of the manhood of our race."

For Martin Delany, Douglass's response fell short of a remedy. It was not enough to challenge the individual kidnapper when the source of the problem was the prejudice that permeated all American institutions,

The harsh measures of the Fugitive Slave Law aroused fear among free blacks living in Northern cities.

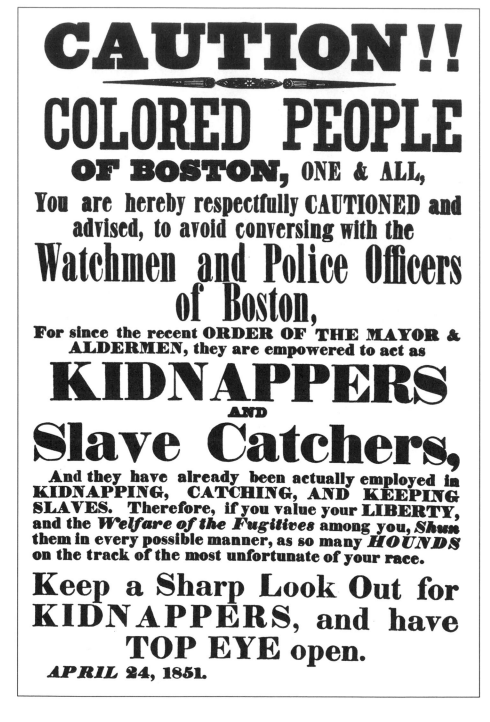

CAUTION!!
COLORED PEOPLE
OF BOSTON, ONE & ALL,

You are hereby respectfully CAUTIONED and advised, to avoid conversing with the

Watchmen and Police Officers of Boston,

For since the recent ORDER OF THE MAYOR & ALDERMEN, they are empowered to act as

KIDNAPPERS
AND
Slave Catchers,

And they have already been actually employed in KIDNAPPING, CATCHING, AND KEEPING SLAVES. Therefore, if you value your LIBERTY, and the *Welfare of the Fugitives* among you, *Shun* them in every possible manner, as so many *HOUNDS* on the track of the most unfortunate of your race.

Keep a Sharp Look Out for KIDNAPPERS, and have TOP EYE open.

APRIL 24, 1851.

An engraving from Harriet Beecher Stowe's Uncle Tom's Cabin *(1852).* Uncle Tom's Cabin *raised public awareness about the evils of slavery.*

including the government. Shoot one kidnapper, and another would take his place. The law was a reflection of government policy, and in Delany's opinion even the call for separate black institutions did not go far enough to counter white racism. When Delany pondered institutional discrimination and the Fugitive Slave Law, he concluded that "a people capable of originating and sustaining such a law as this are not people to whom we are willing to entrust our liberty at discretion." His advice was to "go to whatever parts of Central and South America" and "make common cause with the people." For Delany, emigration was still the only answer.

Delany found support at conventions held in Maryland in 1852 and Cleveland in 1854. Unlike the delegates to the Rochester convention, those who attended the Cleveland meeting were not reluctant supporters of black separatism, nor did they see the point in arguing for separation as a means to American citizenship. As Delany put it, it was time for black people to look outside of America, to grab hold of those places in the world where chance was in their favor and where the rights and power of the colored race could be established.

Although more blacks than ever took up this position in the 1850s, most African Americans remained hopeful of change within the United States. They could not abandon the land of their birth, give up the dream for which their forefathers had sacrificed so much, nor leave their enslaved brethren with no black advocates for freedom. Delegates to the Baltimore convention found this out when the meeting they called to discuss emigration was broken up by angry black crowds who wanted no part of Africa, Haiti, Mexico, or Canada. They did not disagree with the delegates' demand to be treated like men. Nor did they take issue with the convention's general sentiment that in Maryland swine were treated better than free Negroes. Clearly though, they, like most free blacks, wanted to make their stand here in America.

In the first few years of the decade it seemed that they had support. In fact, white Northerners did grow more sympathetic. This was in part because the Fugitive Slave Law brought the issue of slavery to their doorstep. Whites who witnessed slaves being dragged unwillingly back South found it difficult to remain detached from the issue. They could no longer treat it as something that just happened "down there."

And what was happening "down there" was made even more real by the publication in magazine installments, and then as a book in 1852, of Harriet Beecher Stowe's *Uncle Tom's Cabin*. In a brilliant manipulation of public sentiment, Stowe raised public consciousness about the evils of slavery. She did this by making her slaves people with whom almost all whites could identify. There were few Northern mothers who did not hail Eliza's courageous escape across the floes of the Ohio River, or cry over Little Eva's death. Only the meanest could side with the wicked Yankee slaveholder Simon Legree, and all could see the Christlike goodness of the beloved Uncle Tom. So large and so stirred was the northern readership that when Lincoln met Stowe in 1863 he is supposed to have said, "So you're the little woman who wrote the book that made this great war!"

If African Americans had reason to be buoyed by this new awareness on the part of the Northern public, they surely had reason to be wary of the response it drew from Southerners. Already unnerved by the steady economic progress and increasing boldness of free blacks, Southern whites' anxiety only increased in the face of Northern antislavery activity. In particular, slaveholders were sure that free blacks and increased antislavery activity had something to do with the increase in the number of runaway slaves and incidents of overt resistance.

And to Southerners it seemed as though every day brought news of some other violent incident involving slaves. It was said that overseers in the Mississippi Valley so feared for their lives that they were never caught without their guns. In Tennessee four slaves were put to death for attempting to attack the iron mills where they worked. From North Carolina came news of a group of runaways hidden between Bladen and Robeson counties who reportedly were "of bad and daring character—destructive to all kinds of stock and dangerous to all persons living by or near said swamp." The runaways defied the whites who tried to drive them out, boldly "cursing and swearing and telling them to come on, they were ready for them again."

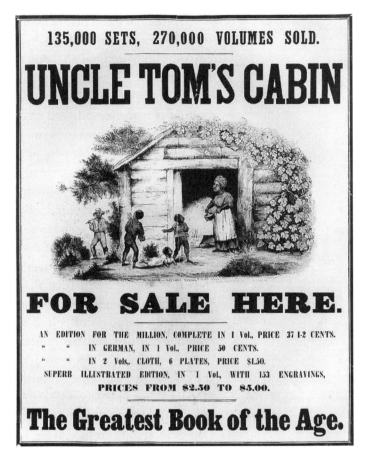

An advertisement for Uncle Tom's Cabin *deems it "the Greatest Book of the Age." The book was a huge success, selling more than 300,000 copies in a single year, and was translated into many foreign languages.*

Some blacks in Texas also seemed ready. From that state came news of a alleged plot that was to bring blacks and Mexicans together in an attempt to rid the state of its white population. Although whites killed five blacks suspected of fomenting the insurrection, they could not quell black discontent, nor white fear of it.

They tried to, though. Because they felt that the ever-growing free-black population was inciting slaves to flee and rebel, Southerners tried to get rid of them. With the exception of Delaware and North Carolina, every Upper South state instituted a colonization plan. Virginia's was typical. In 1850 it appropriated $30,000 annually for five years to send free blacks and emancipated slaves to the West African nation of Liberia.

A tax placed on free blacks added an additional $10,000. Maryland passed a similar law in 1852, Tennessee in 1853, and Missouri and Kentucky in 1855.

These plans failed for two reasons. To begin with, not enough money was appropriated for such a massive removal of people. But even had there been enough funds, there were few people who wanted to go. African Americans were already opposed to the emigration plans proposed by their own leaders. They were hardly more disposed to leaving under a program arranged by their oppressors. John Rapier said what most blacks believed: "They [colonizationists] would not care if all the free negroes in the United States was at the Botom of the Sea so they was out of the United States."

Not only was Rapier right, he caught what was fast becoming the temper of the nation. Everywhere, not just in the South, anti-black sentiment was rising. Indiana offers a good example of this mood. In 1851 state legislators rewrote the state constitution with provisions that deprived blacks of the rights to vote, attend white schools, and make contracts. African Americans who could not post a $500 bond were expelled from the state, and an 1852 law made it a crime for blacks to settle in Indiana.

If nothing else these state laws demonstrated that antislavery sentiment easily coexisted with hostility toward African Americans. Most white citizens did not want *any* blacks in their midst, slave or free. This sentiment found national expression in the new Republican party, which was founded in 1854. The principal platform of this mostly Northern party was "no slavery in the territories." By this Republicans meant that they wanted to keep the new western territories as "free soil," meaning free of slavery. Slavery, they believed, retarded upward mobility and economic growth. From their point of view the South was stagnant and backward, while the North and Upper Midwest were energetic and progressive. Republicans promised not to oppose slavery where it already was. But inasmuch as America's democracy and its institutions depended on the ability of men to move and work in a free labor market, they argued that the future greatness of the American nation depended on the confinement of slavery and the expansion of free soil.

For African Americans the Republican party was both good and bad news. The good news was that many Republicans were abolitionists who opposed not just the expansion of slavery but also slavery where it existed. Senator William Seward of New York and Senators Charles Sumner of Massachusetts and George Julian of Ohio were ardent abolitionists who sought to divorce the federal government from the support of slavery by freeing slaves in the District of Columbia, repealing the Fugitive Slave Law, and eliminating the domestic slave trade.

There was good news too in even the limited goal of keeping slavery out of the territories. The rival party, the Democrats, had already gone on record as supporting popular sovereignty, the settler's right to decide whether slavery should exist in the territories. Its leading politician, Stephen A. Douglas, had pushed the Kansas-Nebraska Act through Congress early in 1854. This act allowed the people who settled in the newly organized Kansas and Nebraska regions to decide for themselves whether they wanted slavery. In allowing for the possibility of slavery in these territories the act overturned the 1820 Missouri Compromise, which had outlawed slavery in regions north of Missouri. The Republicans thus offered a much-needed counter to what was without a doubt a major threat from the power of the slave owners.

The bad news, though, was that the bulk of the party's support came from whites who were as much anti-black as they were antislavery. From the African American's point of view this made the party suspect. Republicans did not directly oppose slavery where it was, nor did they tackle issues like the domestic slave trade or the Fugitive Slave Law. Furthermore, the party's supporters and its prominent leader, Abraham Lincoln, did not favor equal rights for African Americans. In opposing the vote, jury service, and intermarriage, Republicans made clear their belief that whites were superior to blacks, and that the two races could not live together on terms of social and political equality.

The formation of the Republican party, therefore, left blacks with a lot to think about. They took heart that there was, for the first time, a political force opposing slavery, but they worried about the limits of that opposition and the extent to which the Republicans would go to keep blacks from exercising civil and political rights. That they were still without effective national allies in an increasingly hostile environment was a fact that did not escape them.

The depth of the nation's hostility to blacks was revealed by the Supreme Court's 1857 decision in *Scott* v. *Sandford* (the "Dred Scott

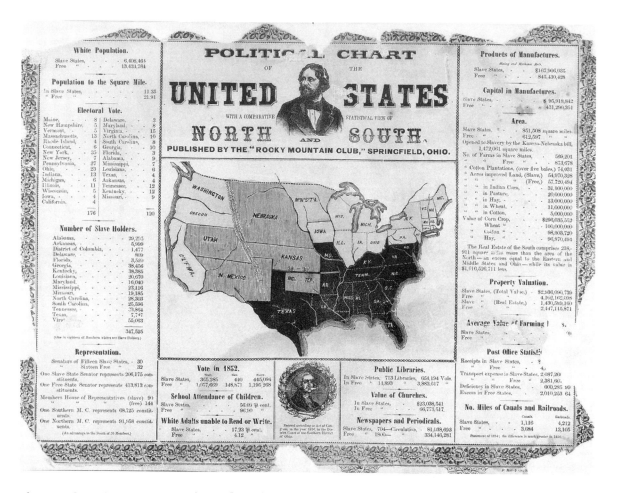

This 1856 chart of the United States shows the division between free and slave states. The chart also offers a statistical comparison between the North and the South, with figures for the number of public libraries, the number of children who attend school, and other categories.

case"), a ruling that sent shivers down the spine of black America. In 1846 Dred and Harriet Scott had filed suit in Missouri for their freedom. They argued that because their master had taken them into Minnesota, Wisconsin, and other territories where slavery had been outlawed by the Missouri Compromise, they were by right free. Chief Justice Roger B. Taney, writing for the court, disagreed. Dred and Harriet Scott were not free. Taney stated that blacks were "beings of an inferior order" and therefore "had no rights which white men were bound to respect." Justice Peter V. Daniel, of Virginia, added insult to injury by his claim that "the African Negro race" did not belong "to the family of nations" but rather was only a subject for "commerce or traffic," "slaves," "property."

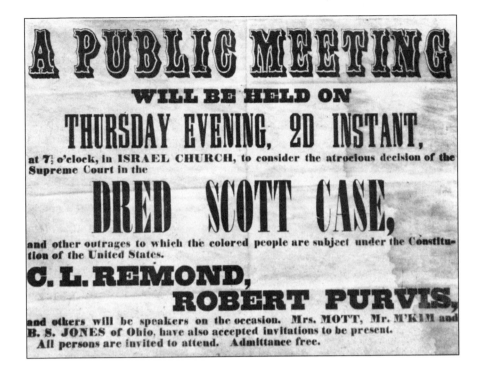

A PUBLIC MEETING

WILL BE HELD ON

THURSDAY EVENING, 2D INSTANT,

at 7½ o'clock, in ISRAEL CHURCH, to consider the atrocious decision of the Supreme Court in the

DRED SCOTT CASE,

and other outrages to which the colored people are subject under the Constitution of the United States.

C. L. REMOND,

ROBERT PURVIS,

and others will be speakers on the occasion. Mrs. MOTT, Mr. M'KIM and B. S. JONES of Ohio, have also accepted invitations to be present. All persons are invited to attend. Admittance free.

The Supreme Court's ruling in the Dred Scott case shocked and outraged free blacks. In Philadelphia, free blacks called a public meeting to discuss their feelings about the case.

If this part of the ruling fell like a dead weight on free blacks, the court's decision regarding the Missouri Compromise was a death sentence. In stating that the 1820 law was unconstitutional because Congress did not have the right to ban slavery in a territory, the court opened the entire country to slavery. If Congress could not ban slavery in the territories then it could not keep it out of northern states. Slaveholders could take their slaves north, settle wherever they wanted, and according to the logic of the Dred Scott decision, there was nothing that could be done about it. When put together with the Fugitive Slave Law, the Dred Scott decision left nowhere for the fugitive to run. Questionable as the North was as a haven for free blacks, these two measures eliminated it as a haven of any sort.

Events in Kansas between 1854 and John Brown's raid at Harpers Ferry, Virginia, in 1859, literally left free blacks nationless. After the Kansas-Nebraska Act was passed both pro- and antislavery forces rushed into Kansas, each group attempting to make sure that the territory was settled according to its wishes. At stake was whether the territories would be slave or free. With both forces willing to die for their cause, violence was inevitable. As the forces clashed in guerrilla-style warfare, only the free blacks' future there was certain: slaveholders did not want them in their midst, and free-soilers wrote a constitution that forbade them from entering the state.

John Brown's raid only made the situation of free blacks more precarious. When the dust settled after the band of 22 men tried to take the federal arsenal at Harpers Ferry, free blacks were found to be among the conspirators. Slaveholders cringed when they thought about what might have happened had Brown's plan to seize and distribute weapons to slaves succeeded. They could and did hang John Brown for treason, but many thousands of free blacks who stood ready to take up Brown's mantle remained among the population. Having always viewed the free black as out of place in the South, white Southerners now saw an opportunity to eliminate this group for good.

Life for Southern free blacks had grown harder and more dangerous. States that had already made efforts to force them to leave through colonization renewed their efforts to eliminate them—this time through outright expulsion. Events in South Carolina, the home of William

John Brown's raid on the federal arsenal at Harpers Ferry, Virginia, in 1859. Ten of Brown's men were killed in the attack. Brown was captured and hanged.

Ellison, were typical. On the urging of Charleston's white mechanics, city officials cracked down on free people of color. In October 1858 they began arresting those who had failed to pay the capitation (literally, "per head") tax, the tax free persons of color had to pay to attest to their freedom. In December of the following year, white Charlestonians formed a Committee of Safety to search out and arrest anyone with abolitionist sympathies. These included whites who ran black schools and blacks who received abolitionist newspapers or otherwise engaged in suspicious behavior. A similar committee was formed by Ellison's neighbors in Stateburg.

Meanwhile, as the state legislature debated reenslavement bills, South Carolina's newspapers carried articles assailing the free African American at every turn. One contributor asked why free blacks were allowed to attend balls, churches, and funerals in carriages; why they were allowed to assume the prerogatives and distinctions that "ought to be, among the landmarks separating the classes." "Shall they," he continued, "in silks and laces, promenade our principal thoroughfares, with the arrogance of equals."

If the white slaveholders who were the guardians of free blacks were willing to put up with such behavior, white workingmen made it clear that they were not. In the South Carolina state legislature their leaders introduced a bill that prohibited all free persons of color from "entering into contracts on any mechanical business on their own account." With a call to "MECHANICS, WORKING MEN AND ALL WHITE MEN WHO LIVE BY THE SWEAT OF THEIR BROW," white workers urged solidarity against free blacks.

William Ellison saw the handwriting on the wall. A master cotton gin-maker who worshipped on the same level of his church as whites, who owned considerable property, including slaves, Ellison was among those who white workers assailed for assuming the distinctions that belonged only to white men. Now, however, the legislature was not only debating whether he and his sons would be able to practice their trade, it was considering returning him, his children, and his grandchildren to slavery.

Along with thousands of other free blacks throughout the South, most of whom were not nearly as wealthy, Ellison and his family made plans to emigrate. First his son sent his children North. A sign of the desperate times was the difficulty they had getting out of South Carolina.

A group of slaves escaping to the North. The Fugitive Slave Law and the Dred Scott decision meant that for escaped slaves, the North was no longer the haven it once was.

Since vigilance committees had made assisting free blacks risky, Ellison Jr. could find no white person who would escort his children to Philadelphia without him signing them over as slaves. Fearful they would indeed slip into real slavery if he sent them this way, Ellison Jr. put his 10-, 12-, and 14-year-old children on a boat to New York with only the promise of the captain to look out for them and make sure they found their way from New York to Philadelphia. Once they were on their way, he, his father, and his brother made plans to sell their land, their homes, their gin shop, and their 59 slaves, and join the steady stream of free blacks heading out of the South.

Between 1858 and the election of Lincoln in 1860, the stream became a river. As in South Carolina, every Southern legislature debated expulsion and reenslavement, and like Ellison, free blacks considered moving either north to Canada or south to Haiti or Central America. It did not matter that by the Civil War only Arkansas had actually expelled free blacks, ordering them to leave the state by January 1, 1860, or be enslaved. The fury with which expulsion and enslavement were being debated scared African Americans. Like Ellison's son-in-law, James M.

Johnson, they felt "it is better to make a sacrifice now than wait to be sacrificed *our selves*."

African-American leaders could not help but be disturbed. Everywhere they looked forces seemed arrayed against their people. Events in Kansas, the Dred Scott decision, the Fugitive Slave Law, expulsion and reenslavement bills all made for despair. The nation was moving toward dissolution with a certainty that was frightening. While free African Americans were being sacrificed, Southern calls for secession threatened to tighten the noose of slavery around blacks forever. So depressed was the ever-optimistic Frederick Douglass that he, like Ellison, began looking toward Haiti as a possible homeland for black people. Martin Delany, who had by Lincoln's election already moved himself, his wife, and his five children to Canada, traveled to West Africa in search of a place for his people to settle.

Amazingly, but understandably, the same events that caused so much despair for free blacks and their leaders seemed to inspire slaves. As they had done during the American Revolution and the War of 1812, slaves turned the nation's turmoil to their advantage. That they were at the center of the nation's divisions did not escape them, because by 1860 the future of slavery was on everyone's mind and lips. The slaves' knowledge was manifested by acts meant to subvert the system. From Austin, Texas, came reports of slaves' attempts to repeat "the horrors enacted at Harpers Ferry." In Montgomery, Alabama, it was reported that Negroes had plotted to divide up the estates, mules, lands, and household furniture of their white masters. While white South Carolinians trembled when they thought about the rumored black secret organization that was bent on freedom and justice, Kentuckians kept close watch on the case of a slave named Isaac, brought to court for attempting to poison his master and the master's wife and child. The more conversations they overheard, the more newspaper articles that literate blacks read, the clearer it became that there were forces beyond the South lining up against slavery.

What was not clear though was the nature and the strength of these forces. The Republicans opposed slavery in the territories, but they also opposed black rights. Their leader, Abraham Lincoln, wavered when it came to African Americans. At one point he spoke in favor of black rights. Blacks, he said are "my equal and . . . the equal of every living man." The Negro man, he declared, is "entitled to all the natural

A poster for the Republican ticket in the 1860 Presidential election. Though Lincoln opposed the expansion of slavery, he was also opposed to granting political and social equality to blacks.

rights . . . in the Declaration of Independence" and had the right also to "put into his mouth the bread that his own hands have earned." At another point, though, Lincoln spoke words that were more in line with most of his generation. He claimed that he was against "the social and political equality of the white and black races," that he did not "favor making voters or jurors of negroes, nor of qualifying them to hold office, nor to intermarry with white people." Since, he said, there was a "physical difference between the white and black races which . . . will for ever forbid the two races living together on terms of social and political equality," Lincoln went on record as favoring whites over blacks. "There must be," he said during his campaign for the Senate in 1858, "the position of superior and inferior, and I as much as any other man am in favor of having the superior position assigned to the white race."

Expressions such as these inspired increasing despair. To Southerners, Abraham Lincoln was the devil incarnate, ready and willing to

snatch their slaves from them at whatever cost. Had African Americans felt this way they would have greeted his election in 1860 with more enthusiasm. Instead his victory was met with caution that only increased when Lincoln refused to move against the seven states (South Carolina, Mississippi, Florida, Alabama, Georgia, Louisiana, and Texas) that established the Confederacy before his inauguration in March 1861. Like Douglass, blacks wanted "the complete and universal *abolition* of the whole slave system," as well as equal suffrage and other rights for free blacks. In early 1861 Lincoln was still promising not to touch slavery where it was and not to repeal the Fugitive Slave Law. Small wonder then that African Americans hardly celebrated his inauguration.

The firing on Fort Sumter, South Carolina, on April 12, 1861 did, however, bring celebration. These first shots of the Civil War stirred real hope that slavery would soon end. It all happened so suddenly, soon after the officer in charge of the fort, Major Robert Anderson, informed Lincoln that he needed men, arms, and supplies to maintain the federal presence in Charleston harbor. Lincoln's dilemma was obvious. If he did

The Civil War began on April 12, 1861, when Confederate forces fired on Fort Sumter, South Carolina.

nothing, he would appear weak and Sumter would fall to the Confederacy, as had other federal forts, custom houses, and post offices. On the other hand, if he sent forces this would no doubt be taken by the Confederacy as an act of war. Lincoln's choice—to send supplies but no troops or arms—shifted the burden of war to the Confederacy, which itself stood to lose credibility as a sovereign nation if it allowed Lincoln to maintain the fort within its borders. It was hardly their intention, but the shots Confederate generals fired on the ships sent to resupply Anderson were shots that put slavery on the road to extinction.

The firing on Fort Sumter, therefore, brought real jubilation to African Americans. No matter that Lincoln had sought to avoid war by sending only food and supplies to Major Anderson, or that the Republicans delayed until 1863 their decision to make the war a war against slavery. No matter, either, that throughout the conflict Lincoln searched for ways to colonize black people in Costa Rica and Liberia. African Americans knew in 1861 what Lincoln and the nation at the time could not even fathom:

> Slavery chain done broke at last!
> Broke at last! Broke at last!
> Slavery chain done broke at last!
> Gonna praise God till I die!

CHRONOLOGY

◇ ◇ ◇

1800

Gabriel Prosser's planned revolt against slavery in Virginia fails; Prosser and his followers are hanged.

1808

The foreign slave trade is closed. Africans are no longer legally imported into the United States.

1811

Led by enslaved leader Charles Deslondes, about 400 enslaved blacks revolt and flee plantations in St. John and St. Charles Parishes in Louisiana.

1816

The American Colonization Society is formed by white Americans. Their aim is to send African Americans back to Africa. Few blacks support the program.

1817-18

African Americans join the Seminole Indians in their fight to keep their Florida homelands.

1820

The Missouri Compromise allows Missouri to enter the United States as a slave state but outlaws slavery north of the 36°30' parallel.

1822

Denmark Vesey, a free African American, plans a revolt against the arsenal at Charleston and surrounding plantations. He is betrayed before the revolt begins. Vesey and his followers are hanged.

1822

The American Colonization Society buys land in western Africa for the few blacks who want to return. The nation is called Liberia.

1827

Freedom's Journal, the first African-American newspaper, is published by Samuel Cornish and John Russworm.

1829

David Walker issues his *Appeal* in which he denounces slavery and calls on African Americans to rise up and throw off the yoke of slavery.

1829

More than half of the black people of Cincinnati flee the city in response to white mob violence. Riots in other north-ern and western cities force blacks to migrate to Canada and elsewhere.

1830

African-American delegates from New York, Pennsylvania, Maryland, Delaware, and Virginia meet in Philadelphia in what was the first of many conventions to devise ways of bettering the condition of free and enslaved blacks.

1831

Nat Turner leads about 70 fellow slaves in uprising against the slaveholders of Southampton, Virginia. He and his followers are captured and hanged but not before killing about 60 whites.

1833

The predominantly white American Anti-Slavery Society is formed, signalling the beginning of organized white protest against slavery.

1835

Fugitive slaves join the Seminoles against the militias of Florida, Georgia, and Tennessee to keep their homelands.

1847

Renowned black abolitionist Frederick Douglass publishes abolitionist newspaper the *North Star*.

1850

The Compromise of 1850 is passed with the most repressive fugitive slave law ever passed in the United States.

1852

Black activist and abolitionist Martin Delany publishes *The Condition, Elevation, Emigration, and Destiny of the Colored People of the United States* in which he argues that emigration to Central or South America or some area in the American west offers the best prospects for black freedom.

1854

The Republican Party is formed on the premise that slavery must be kept out of the western territories. Southerners are threatened by the party's position.

1857

In *Scott* v. *Sandford,* the Supreme Court rules that blacks are not citizens and therefore have no legal rights; that blacks are property, and whites who possess such property can treat them however they please and can take them wherever they want.

1859

White abolitionist John Brown leads a slave revolt against the federal arsenal at Harpers Ferry, Virginia. Brown is captured and hanged. Revolt spreads fear among slaveholders across the nation.

1860

Arkansas expels all free blacks from the state. Other Southern states had debated expulsion of free blacks but only Arkansas passes an expulsion law.

1860

Abraham Lincoln is elected President on the Republican platform of non-extension of slavery. Seven Southern states secede in reaction to his election.

APRIL 12, 1861

Civil war begins when Confederates fire on a United States ship sent to re-supply Fort Sumter, in South Carolina, with food and supplies. Six more Southern states secede and join the Confederacy.

FURTHER READING

◇ ◇ ◇

GENERAL AFRICAN-AMERICAN HISTORY

Bennett, Lerone, Jr. *Before the Mayflower: A History of Black America.* 6th rev. ed. New York: Viking Penguin, 1988.

———. *The Shaping of Black America.* New York: Viking Penguin, 1993.

Foner, Philip S. *History of Black Americans: From Africa to the Emergence of the Cotton Kingdom.* Westport, Conn.: Greenwood, 1975.

Franklin, John Hope, and Alfred A. Moss. *From Slavery To Freedom. A History of Negro Americans.* 7th ed. New York: Knopf, 1994.

Gates, Henry L., Jr. *A Chronology of African-American History from 1445–1980.* New York: Amistad, 1980.

Giddings, Paula. *When and Where I Enter: The Impact of Black Women on Race and Sex in America.* New York: Bantam, 1985.

Harding, Vincent. *There Is a River: The Black Struggle for Freedom in America.* San Diego: Harcourt Brace, 1981.

Hine, Darlene C., et al., eds. *Black Women in America.* Brooklyn, N.Y.: Carlson, 1993.

Levine, Lawrence. *Black Culture and Black Consciousness: Afro-American Folk Thought from Slavery to Freedom.* New York: Oxford, 1977.

Litwack, Leon and August Meier. *Black Leaders of the 19th Century.* Urbana: University of Illinois Press, 1988.

Meltzer, Milton. *The Black Americans: A History in Their Own Words.* Rev. ed. New York: HarperCollins, 1984.

Mintz, Sidney W. and Richard Price. *The Birth of African-American Culture: An Anthropological Perspective.* Boston: Beacon Press, 1992.

Nash, Gary B. and Julie R. Jeffrey. *The American People: Creating a Nation and a Society.* 2nd ed. New York: Harper-Collins, 1990.

Quarles, Benjamin. *The Negro in the Making of America.* 3rd ed. New York: Macmillan, 1987.

SLAVERY AND PLANTATION LIFE

Berlin, Ira. *Slaves Without Masters: The Free Negro in the Antebellum South.* New York: Random House, 1974.

Blassingame, John W. *The Slave Community: Plantation Life in the Antebellum South.* Rev. ed. New York: Oxford University Press, 1979.

Botkin, B. A., ed. *Lay My Burden Down: A Folk History of Slavery.* Chicago: University of Chicago Press, 1945.

Genovese, Eugene. *Roll, Jordan, Roll: The World the Slaves Made.* New York: Random House, 1974.

Gutman, Herbert. *The Black Family in Slavery and Freedom, 1750–1925.* New York: Pantheon, 1976.

Johnson, Michael and James L. Roark. *Black Masters: A Free Family of Color in the Old South*. New York: Norton, 1984.

Kolchin, Peter. *American Slavery 1619–1877*. New York: Hill & Wang, 1993.

Lebsock, Suzanne. *The Free Women of Petersburg: Status and Culture in a Southern Town, 1784–1860*. New York: Norton, 1984.

Litwack, Leon F. *North of Slavery: The Negro in the Free States, 1790–1860*. Chicago: University of Chicago Press, 1961.

Meier, August and Elliot M. Rudwick. *From Plantation to Ghetto: An Interpretive History of American Negroes*. 3rd ed. New York: Hill and Wang, 1976.

Nash, Gary B. *Forging Freedom: The Formation of Philadelphia's Black Community, 1720–1840*. Cambridge: Harvard, 1988.

Osofsky, Gilbert, ed. *Puttin' On Ole Massa. The Slave Narratives of Henry Bibb, William Wells Brown and Solomon Northup*. New York: Harper & Row, 1969.

Richardson, Marilyn, ed. *Maria W. Stewart, America's First Black Woman Political Writer: Essays and Speeches*. Bloomington: Indiana, 1987.

Sweet, Leonard L. *Black Images of America, 1784–1870*. New York: Norton, 1976.

White, Deborah Gray. *Ar'n't I a Woman? Female Slaves in the Plantation South*. New York: Norton, 1985.

Williamson, Joel. *New People: Miscegenation and Mulattoes in the United States*. New York: Free Press, 1980.

BIOGRAPHIES AND AUTOBIOGRAPHIES

Andrews, William L., ed. *The Oxford Frederick Douglass Reader*. New York: Oxford University Press, 1996.

Bentley, Judith. *Harriet Tubman*. New York: Franklin Watts, 1990.

Douglass, Frederick. *Narrative of the Life of Frederick Douglass, an American Slave*. New York: St. Martin's Press, 1993.

Edwards, Lillie J. *Denmark Vesey*. New York: Chelsea House, 1990.

Gilbert, Olive. *Narrative of Sojourner Truth*. New York: Oxford University Press, 1991.

Klots, Steve. *Richard Allen: Founder of the African Methodist Episcopal Church*. New York: Chelsea House, 1990.

Krass, Peter. *Sojourner Truth*. New York: Chelsea House, 1988.

McFeely, William S. *Frederick Douglass*. New York: Norton, 1991.

Miller, Douglas T. *Frederick Douglass and the Fight for Freedom*. New York: Facts on File, 1988.

INDEX

◇ ◇ ◇

References to illustrations are indicated by page numbers in *italics*.

Affleck, Thomas, 49
African Episcopal Church of St. Thomas, *91*
African Methodist Episcopal Church, 92
Allston, Adele Pettigru, 59-60
Allston, Robert, 32
American Anti-Slavery Almanac, 116
American Antislavery Society, 99, 101, 108
American Colonization Society, 102, 103, *104*
American Revolution, 76-77
Anderson, Elijah, 120
Anderson, Robert, 135
Anti-Slavery Alphabet, The, 102
Anti-Slavery Record, The, 67

Bacchus, Josephine, 54
Baltimore, Maryland, 91-92, 118
Bell, Phillip A., 114-15
Bible Defense of Slavery, 22
Black codes, 85, 119
Black press, 110-14
Black separatism, 114-15, 120
Bomefree, Isabella. *See* Truth, Sojourner
Botts, Ellen, 49
Br'er Rabbit, 39, 40
Brown Fellowship Society, 94
Brown, Henry "Box," 61, *62*
Brown, John, 30, 60

Brown, William Wells, 111
Burns, Anthony, 120

Certificates of freedom, *72,* 84, 85
Charleston, South Carolina, 94, 118, 130
Cherokees, 17
Chesnut, Mary Boykin, 49-50
Chickasaws, 17
Choctaws, 17
Cincinnati Colonization Society, 108
Clay, Henry, 102
Cocke, John Hartwell, 32-34
Coker, Daniel, 91
Colored American, The, 111, 112
Committee of 1850, 130
Compromise of 1850, 117
Condition, Elevation, Emigration, and Destiny of the Colored People of the United States, The (Delaney), 113-14
Cotton, 8, 15-17, *24, 25*
planting and cultivation of, 25
Cotton gin, 8, 15, *16,* 18
Covey, Edward, 57-58
Craft, Ellen, 61-62
Craft, William, 62
Creeks, 17
Cuffee, Paul, 104
Cunningham, Adeline, 19-20
Curfews, 84

Daniel, Peter, 127-28
Delany, Martin, 111, 112, 113-14, 118, 120, 122, 132

Deslondes, Charles, 68-69
Douglass, Frederick, 8, 52, 57-61, 83-84, 97, 99, 101, 109-10, 111, 112-13, 118, 120, 132
Douglas, Stephen, 126
Drivers, 32, 34-35

Ellison, April. *See* Ellison, William (formerly April)
Ellison, Eliza Ann, 73
Ellison, Matilda, 73
Ellison, William, 73
Ellison, William (formerly April), 73, 77-81, 88, 94, 95, 97, 118, 130-31
Emancipation laws, 76

Folk tales, 7
Forten, James, 18, 103
Forten, Margaretta, 88
Fort Sumter, South Carolina, *134,* 135
Frazier, Rossana, 54
Free African Society, 88
Free blacks, 8-9, 18, 73-97
as barbers, 87
benevolent societies among, 92, 94-95
children, 88
class structure among, 96
as contract laborers, 79
economic opportunities for, 87
education of, 91-92
as farmers, 79
legal restrictions on, 84-86
legal rights of, 88
mobility of, 78-79
name changes by, 77
opposition to coloni-

zation schemes, 102-7, 124-25
opposition to slavery, 100-8
population of, 76-77, 82
religious practices of, 88-91
relationship with white abolitionists, 107-10
skin color among, 80, 94-96
threat to white labor, 83-84
as urban dwellers, 81-83
violence against, *86,* 87
women, 87, 95
See also Mulattoes
Freedom's Journal, 94, 104, *107*
Free Soil, 125
Friendly Moralist Society, 94
Fugitive slave laws, 101-2, 117
Fugitive Slave Law of 1850, 117, 120, *121,* 122, 123, 126, 128, 134
Fugitive's Song, The, 56

Gantling, Clayborn, 31
Garnet, Henry Highland, 8, 111
Garrison, William Lloyd, 108, 109
Georgia Sea Islands, 7-8, 15
Green, Charles, 77
Griggs, Aaron, 79
Gullah Jack, 70

Hall, Prince, 92
Harpers Ferry, Virginia, 128-29
Harper, William, 22-23

Henrico County, Virginia, 13
Hughes, Louis, 49
Humane Brotherhood, 94, 95
Hundley, Daniel R., 32

Jackson, Andrew, 69, 102
Jacobs, Harriet Brent, 43, 63-64
Jamestown, Virginia, 10
Jennings, Elizabeth, 119
Jesup, Thomas, 69-70
Johnson, Benjamin, 64-65
Johnson, Jane, 35
Johnson, Richard, *81*
Jones, Absalom, 88, *90*, 101
Jones, Charles C., 54
Jones, John and Mary, *119*
Julian, George, 126

Kansas-Nebraska Act, 126, 128-29
Keckley, Elizabeth Hobbs, 73-74, 87, 95, 118
Keckley, James, 73-75
Kemble, Frances, 45, 75
Key, Frances Scott, 102
Kinney, Nicey, 54

Latrobe, John B., 103, *104*
Liberia, 103-04, *105, 106*
Liberator, The, 109
Liberty Party, 99
Lincoln, Abraham, 118, 123, *133*, 133-35
Lincoln, Mary Todd, 75
Loguen, Jermaine, 65
Lundy, Benjamin, 108

Madison, James, 102
Manumission, 73-74, 95
Mason, Henry, 77
Mason, John, 120
Mexican War, 100
Missouri Compromise, 83, 126, 127, 128
Moore, Fannie, 48
Morgan, John H., 67
Moses, the Baltimore News Vendor (Wood), *87-88*
Mulattoes, 80, *81*, 94-95

New England Antislavery Society, 108

New Era, The, 111
New York Free African School, *93*
New York Society for Promoting the Manumission of Slaves, *93*
North Star, 98, 99
Northup, Solomon, 18, 31-32
Northwest Ordinance of 1787, 85

Ohio Black Laws, 108

Pendleton, E. M., 67
Penn, William, 63
Philadelphia Vigilance Committee, 63
Polk, James K., 30
Poyas, Peter, 70
Prosser, Gabriel, 8, 13, 17, 23, 70
Prosser, Martin, 13
Prosser, Nanny, 13
Prosser, Solomon, 13

Rapier, John, 125
Re-enslavement bills, 130-32
Republican Party, 125-126, 132-33
Reynolds, Mary, 61
Richmond Enquirer, 19
Richmond Examiner, 14
Russwurm, John, 94, 104

Saratoga Street African Methodist Episcopal Church, 91
Scott, Dred, 127-28
Scott, Hannah, 49
Scott, Harriet, 127-28
Scott v. *Sandford* (1857), *127-28, 129*
Seminoles, 17, 68-69, *69*
Seward, William, 126
Simpson, Ben, 32
Sims, Thomas, 120
Skipwith, George, 32, 34
Slave codes, 36-37
Slave community, 21, 37, 39-55
   conjurers, 53-54, 58
   education of children, 47-48

folk beliefs within, 52-54
folk tales of, 39-40, 48, 55
importance of silence in, 40
medicine, 54-55
music within, 50-52
religion, 49-52, *50, 53, 55*, 62
Slave patrols, 60, *61*
Slavery,
   "abroad marriage," 65
   arguments for, 21-23
   birth and death rates in, 20, 21, 44
   birth control, 66-67
   black opposition to, 8, 97, 99-115
   courtship patterns, 46-47
   daily life under, 8-9, 25-37
   diet, 59-60
   domestic trade, 17-19
   effect of cotton on, 15-17
   escape, 57-59, *58*, 60-64, 124, *131*
   family structure under, 43, 44-49, 65
   gang system, 28
   housework, 28-29
   improved conditions in, 20-21, 71
   infanticide, *67*, 68
   in Lower South, 19-20
   mutual dependence within, 41, 43
   overseers and drivers, 32-33
   physical punishment, 31-33, *33-34*, 35
   plantation size, 29
   political crisis caused by, 117-35
   rebellions, 68-71, 132-33
   resistance to, 57-71
   revolts against, 13, 15
   stealing, 59-60
   task system, 28
   truancy, 64-66
   violent opposition to, 60, 124
   women under, *26*, 30-31,

43, 45, 63-68
   See also Slave codes; Slave community; Slave patrols; Underground Railroad
Smith, Gerrit, 108
Smith, James McCune, 106
Smith, Lou, 68
Smith, Thomas, 77
Southampton, Virginia, 71
Springfellow, Thornton, 23
Stewart, Maria, 8, 18, 111, 112
Still, William, 63
Stowe, Harriet Beecher, 123
Sumner, Charles, 126

Taney, Roger, 127
Tappan, Arthur, 108
Tappan, Lewis, 108
Tar Baby, 39
Terill, J. W., 30
Tobacco, 15
Tredegar Iron Works, 27
Truth, Sojourner, *74*, 75, 76, 77, 88, 118
Tubman, Harriet, 62-63, *63*, 120
Turner, Nat, 8, *70*, 70-71
Turner, West, 35

Uncle Tom's Cabin (Stowe), *122*, 123, *124*
Underground Railroad, 63

Vesey, Denmark, 8, 70-71, 106

Walker, David, 8, 111-12
Walker's Appeal . . ., 111-12, *113*
Watkins, William, 108
Watson, Henry, 36
Webster, Daniel, 102
Weekly Advocate, The, 111, 114-15
Weekly Anglo-African, 111
Whipper, William, 111
Whitney, Eli, 8, 15
Williams, Nancy, 51-52
Williams, Peter, *103*, 108
Williams, Rose, 45
Wolf, 39, 40
Wright, Theodore, 108-9

PICTURE CREDITS

◇ ◇ ◇

DEBORAH GRAY WHITE

◇ ◇ ◇

Deborah Gray White is professor of history at Rutgers University. She holds a Ph.D. from the University of Illinois at Chicago. Dr. White is the author of *"Ar'n't I A Woman?" Female Slaves in the Plantation South*, for which she won the Letitia Brown Memorial Book Prize, and the forthcoming *Too Heavy a Load: Ideas of Race, Class, and Gender in Black Women's History*. She has also contributed articles to *Before Freedom Came: African-American Life in the Antebellum South*, and *Visible Women: New Essays on American Activism*.

ROBIN D.G. KELLEY

◇ ◇ ◇

Robin D. G. Kelley is professor of history and Africana studies at New York University. He previously taught history and African-American studies at the University of Michigan. He is the author of *Hammer and Hoe: Alabama Communists during the Great Depression*, which received the Eliot Rudwick Prize of the Organization of American Historians and was named Outstanding Book on Human Rights by the Gustavus Myers Center for the Study of Human Rights in the United States. Professor Kelley is also the author of *Race Rebels: Culture, Politics, and the Black Working Class* and co-editor of *Imagining Home: Class, Culture, and Nationalism in the African Diaspora*.

EARL LEWIS

◇ ◇ ◇

Earl Lewis is professor of history and Afroamerican studies at the University of Michigan. He served as director of the university's Center for Afroamerican and African Studies from 1990 to 1993. Professor Lewis is the author of *In Their Own Interests: Race, Class and Power in Twentieth Century Norfolk* and co-author of *Blacks in the Industrial Age: A Documentary History*.